A MUSICIAN AND HIS WIFE

VIEW FROM THE DE KOVEN VILLA, FLORENCE

A MUSICIAN
AND HIS WIFE

BY

MRS. REGINALD DE KOVEN

ILLUSTRATED

HARPER & BROTHERS PUBLISHERS
NEW YORK AND LONDON
MCMXXVI

CONTENTS

ILLUSTRATIONS

vii

ILLUSTRATIONS

A MUSICIAN AND HIS WIFE

A MUSICIAN
AND HIS WIFE

CHAPTER ONE

ANCESTRY AND PIONEER DAYS IN THE WEST

MY father's name, Farwell, was originally Favelle, of Norman derivation, and his earliest recorded ancestor followed the Conqueror when he came to rule the Island of Imperial Destiny. Gallic imagination, balanced by Teutonic reason, was one of the qualities contributed by the Normans and the Saxons to the English race, and, as I delight to reflect, it was the inheritance of our distant forbears.

In the seventeenth century English Farwells lived in Devonshire and Somersetshire. They were landowners and often intermarried with members of the peerage. Many took orders and attained high dignities in the Church of England. Hyl-Bishop is the clerical-sounding name of one of the Farwell manor houses in Devonshire, which bears the arms of the family. An Arthur Farwell came to the Colonies as secretary and companion to the Duke of Albemarle in 1687.

A wax bust, life-like in size and in apparent excellence of portraiture, is preserved in the London Museum (once Stafford House) of a certain Mistress

1

Farwell, wife of John, who during the sixteenth century held office in London. Among the members of the family, which is still extant in England, is the well-known barrister Sir George Farwell, author of *A Concise Treatise on Powers* (London, 1874).

In the seventeenth century there lived in Devonshire another Sir George and his wife, Lady Mary, daughter of the Duke of Norfolk, and to them were born twenty-four children. The name Henry appears among the immediate descendants of Sir George, but is not to be found on any of the burial stones of the family in the Devonshire churchyards. Concurrent dates and the negative affirmative of this undiscovered tombstone suggest that he might, indeed, have been that original Henry who came to the American colony. The tombstone of Henry Farwell, who was my father's direct ancestor, has been standing these nearly three hundred years in the Concord churchyard in Massachusetts. Here he was registered in 1635 and here found his wife, Olive. Here, also, he became a "selectman" in the transferred Tun Moot of the Saxon forests, the town meeting of Concord's center of pure democracy, where he floated first his modest standard of civic responsibility which his descendants have faithfully followed.

His son, moving to the stockaded border town of Dunstable, near the joined edges of Massachusetts and New Hampshire, fought the Indians who swarmed about the wooden barrier between the town and the haunted forest. Five Farwells fought in the company of "Roger's Rangers," famous for daringly skillful forest skirmishes in the French and Indian War, and

2

their colonel's wife was a Farwell sister. A Farwell was on Washington's bodyguard; Abraham Farwell was on that famous fatal green of Lexington, foot to foot with a cousin Jackson, relative of my father's mother, who later took command at Concord Bridge. The Jackson strain goes back to a London merchant whose descendants settled in Westminster, now Cambridge, and the Jackson who held the bridge at Concord had as many as forty Jackson cousins enrolled in the little New England army.

Another Henry Farwell of Groton, whither the numerous Farwells had migrated from Dunstable, is thus memorialized on the wall of a red-brick house by a Groton roadside corner. "On the site of this house lived Captain Henry Farwell, who commanded a company of Minute Men at Bunker Hill. Desperately wounded, he was being carried from the field, when he uttered these memorable words: 'I am not dead—and shall not die till I see my country free.' "

Married for the third time at seventy-three, our redoubtable forbear who, it is said, was "of small stature but exceedingly active," lived, according to his promise, to rejoice at the liberty of his victorious country and to become the inspiring influence, as related in Colonial chronicles, of the patriotic ardor and activities of his town and county.

From such examples of upstanding character and courage came, doubtless, the opinion of one of the Revolutionary generals, "that with a company of such soldiers he would be able to drive the enemy into the

3

ocean." This is the family tradition and I hope I may be forgiven for including it in this truthful record.

The genealogical records of the family, as they spread down from the seventeenth to the beginning of the nineteenth century, contain the names of Farwells who were generals and of others who, in correspondence with Jefferson, carried charitable projects as far as Canada. Toward the end of the eighteenth century another Henry Farwell, of Fitchburg, near Groton, married his cousin Hepsibah Farwell of Groton, and their son Henry was my father's father. Later, this Henry Farwell, with his wife, Nancy Jackson of Westminster, moved to the tiny agricultural hamlet called Painted Post in the State of New York. Eclectic in their wants were the inhabitants of Painted Post, if one may judge of them by the sign, proudly displayed on its only mart of trade, which announced that there might be purchased "Cedar posts, white satin and tar." Farming was the sole occupation of the purchasers, whose fields surrounded the Painted Post, and farming was the business of Henry Farwell and of his growing sons, of whom my father, Charles Benjamin, was the second born. Although Charles gathered something more than the rudiments of an education at the neighboring Elmira Academy, he was the acknowledged expert among his brothers and neighbors at the plow and in stacking hay or corn, and so he remained when with his parents he trekked the intervening miles across the wide continent, in a covered wagon called a "prairie schooner," to the new home in Illinois in 1839. When this unit in the constantly advancing army of westward-faring pioneers

4

ventured thus bravely into an arduous and doubtful future in the Middle West, no railroads provided transport; thus only by country roads, across mountains and hundreds of miles of forest and plain, did the "prairie schooner" of Henry Farwell and his family make its slow progress toward the setting sun. The family consisted of father and mother, four sons and a daughter.

Henry Farwell, my grandfather, I saw in my earliest childhood. Like a half-effaced silhouette, with his tall stooping figure, he appears among my memories. He was sad and very quiet, like a tired wayfarer at the close of a toilsome journey. His portrait shows a high, almost dome-like head, indicating courage and imagination. The eyes in the portrait are nearly extinguished, but the nobly cut and regular features are instinct with profound goodness and simplicity. Enterprise he must have had to make the long "trail" from the East to the West, and much courage.

But in courage he was constantly supported by Nancy, his wife, to whose indomitable cheerfulness and humorous common sense my father testified with never changing gratitude and deepest affection. It was she who made the long journey a voyage of enchantment, she who taught her children to see the beauty of field and forest, of dawn and sunset, and the free life of the open road.

So at last they arrived at a farming center called Mount Morris, not many miles from the predestined spot, at the junction of the Illinois River and Lake Michigan, called Chicago, and already, with its few

5

wooden houses clustering around the half-ruined Fort Dearborn, ambitiously calling itself a town.

At Mount Morris, the first work of father and sons was to build, with their own hands, the log cabin, their first home in the West, and next, to cut down the trees and clear their selected acres for farming. Malaria, the pest of the half-cleared country, attacked them, and there were years of struggle with cold and with poverty, the boys learning to make their own shoes, and outside on the farm, as inside at household tasks, aiding their parents in their arduous labor.

From those far-distant years, few family records remain to tell of conditions in the new country. But time then strode in "seven league boots" and for those of this very typical American family who had the courage to adapt their step to its measure, amazing results were at hand. One life, beginning in the virgin forests and ending in the hurrying streets of a great city, might span centuries of ordinary progress. At first, the prospects of Henry Farwell, the farmer, seemed modest enough. With grimmest toil he and his sons cleared the land and sowed their crops, which brought slow and scanty returns. Yet, after a while the log cabin was abandoned for a small red-brick house, which still stands among the surrounding farm lands. In the intervals of farm work, and during the deep snows of winter, Charles learned and practiced surveying, thus fixing the boundaries of the farming lands for the settlers. It was the day of "squatter sovereignty," but limits were needful to form the basis of land titles. How important this work was for his neighbors was soon to be proved. With

6

government papers, there descended upon the region of Mount Morris men who declared themselves agents for the redistribution of the land. The story of the manner in which the farmers met the threat of dispossession was related to me by an eye witness, Mr. Robert R. Hitt, some fifty years later in Washington. No idea existed in the mind of any one of the threatened landholders of giving up their property. But some one had to be selected to be their spokesman, and that one was my nineteen-year-old father. Alone, but backed up by the desperate group of farmers, he met the agents. No violence was used, and none was necessary, for such force was expressed in his words of calm defiance, such decision shone from those clear eyes of youth, that the agents peacefully retreated, leaving the settlers in undisturbed possession of the limits and boundaries which their spokesman and defender had himself determined. Possession, based on the earlier and hitherto undisputed rights of the settlers, proved and justified by the years of cruel toil which had turned forests into fruitful farm lands, was title enough, in those days of newly born government regulations, and so the central government in Washington must have concluded, for no further attempts of dispossession were thereafter made in Mount Morris.

The occupation of surveying the snow-covered fields was varied by hunting deer by moonlight, a rare sport for the boys. But their elders, as in New England, found pleasure in religion. Both father and mother were imbued with the simple faith of the warm Methodist sect, and soon they took their part in gatherings in the cabins of their neighbors, for prayer, exhortation, and song. Here and then was born the religious ardor of my uncle John, which to the end of his life was the guiding motive of a long career of successful activity and enterprise in religious organizations, carried on simultaneously with his business operations. It was he who sent the great revivalists, Moody and Sankey, to England—he who founded the Y. M. C. A. in Chicago, and in Farwell Hall instituted for men of business the "Noon Day Prayer Meeting."

No record remains of my father's participation in these early religious meetings in Mount Morris, but it was he who took their wheat crops to the Chicago market. Thus, on a load of wheat, the young man of twenty rode into the little town whose political life he was destined to rule and also to represent during many years, in Washington, as member of Congress and United States Senator.

Very quickly wheat-selling in the rapidly growing Chicago led to a permanent residence there. Soon he found employment in the bank of the town, as teller and confidential friend of George Smith, whose vast fortune grew from this small Western foundation. Purchases of land were made by my father with his first savings after he had paid a note for his father and bought a cooking stove for his mother.

Long after his death, in an old red pocketbook, I found three papers, very typical of his career and character. One was the record of his first purchase of land, another the canceled note of his father, and the third was a letter from his employer, George Smith. This, in beautiful handwriting, testified, to all who would know, that Charles B. Farwell had the three requisites of success—integrity, ability and courtesy. When, after his almost magical career, the aged banker retired to his one room in the Reform Club in London, my father, then United States Senator, there visited him, and the two men talked of the little bank and youthful beginnings in little Chicago.

Little Chicago it was not destined long to remain. At the juncture of river and the great lake which transported the harvests of the richly fertile surrounding prairies, a favorable point of distribution and rapidly developing trade, the town grew like a young giant. One can imagine Chicago in those days, with its rows of wooden dwellings and stores, rising as rapidly as card houses, its wooden pavements covered with snow and ice in winter and liquid with mud in the breaking spring. The blue lake, filled with carrying steamers, sent its breezes over prairie and town. Nothing was thought of but business, and in this my father soon played his part. Intensely vital, vigorous as an oak of the forests he felled, enterprising and of great mental force, but lucid and logical, he was endowed with the precious gift of personal charm. This combination soon made him a leader among the able men who were destined to build the great city. His mind grew in force and in flexibility like a bird finding its wings. Letters to his favorite brother John show a suddenly developed grace of language, a wit, almost romantic in its youthful enthusiasm, its playful invitation to come away from the farm and join him in his flight to fortune. These letters, in fact,

9

are no longer young, except in enthusiasm, and bear no mark of any pioneer roughness or crudeness of expression. They show, in their delicacy of feeling the persistence of good blood, of ancient and honorable lineage, finding their way at last, like a submerged river, up to the open. Such noble endowments of generosity and humanity, such instincts of "ability and courtesy," soon found their honorable uses. My father was elected clerk of the County of Cook, and in this office, with a circle of chosen associates, established the actual rule of Chicago's government.

It was again Mr. Hitt, my father's Mount Morris friend, who told me of Chicago and its first political leader. As a young reporter Mr. Hitt had learned stenography, and he it was who, for the first time in history, practiced it in the Cook County court-room when my father was clerk.

"When I used to come to Chicago," he said, "your father was all there was of a city government; his word was law and everybody loved him."

A photograph of the city governor surrounded by a group of his friends, showed him in his later twenties, erect, bearded, smiling, with keen eyes under straight brows and the dome-like head of his father, the head of the empire builder. "Empire builders" were the pioneers of this period of almost fabulous expansion, and by reason of his early rule of the great midland city my father also, among his peers, fulfilled this destiny. The keen eyes expressed his clarity and independence of thought, and the warmest of handclasps and a resonant laugh revealed his humanity. He never uttered a harsh word or unjust criticism and was melting wax to misfortune. Built on large lines, both physically and mentally, the proportions of his six feet of manhood were well-nigh perfect. During all his life, all who knew him were impressed by his dignity of bearing. So marked was his head, the typical head of the statesman, that years after his death, when a cartoonist sought for the noblest type he could find among the photographs preserved in Washington, of the legislators of his period, to use in contrast with the far inferior faces, which, as the American stock has become diluted with foreign immigration, have taken their predecessors' places in the halls of Congress, it was the picture of this Senator from northern Illinois which he chose among all others.

Nature, consenting to unite in one personality the best traits of his parents, had added the instinct of taste, which expressed itself in harmony of voice and grace of manner, and also in his use of words. This was indeed remarkable for its brevity and choice. Early he realized the beauty of simplicity, and the simplicity of beauty. "Never too many words," I can hear him say, as he commented with delight upon a favorite orator, "but each one weighing a ton." In the early 'fifties, when he became county clerk and the honored ruler of the rapidly growing Chicago, he dressed with the simple perfection which so well became him—wearing no jewels or rings, but in garments made in New York, sometimes even wearing what was then the last note of fashion, a white high hat. Thus appareled, the most attractive "boss" and the cleanest who ever walked the streets of Chicago, gave to that city the best government in its history.

Independence of thought was perhaps his most remarkable trait. He refused to accept borrowed information, but determined to find out the truth for himself.

He was docile at first in his religious observances through affectionate obedience to his parents, and deeply idealistic in his ethical sense, but resented sentimentalism and, even more sturdily, anything like intellectual slavery. A critical turning point in his attitude toward religion occurred very early in his life in Chicago, when a Methodist Sunday-school teacher declared, with his hand on the Bible, that "he should believe every word in this book before he had opened it." This to my father was like the lash of a slave driver, and soon in full revolt he questioned the Bible and all that his parents believed. Dire rumors of atheism and of certain damnation spread back to the farm, bringing letters of agonized protest from father and mother. From the far-distant region of Painted Post in New York loving old friends sent reams of argument and persuasion to the apostate, penned with genuine concern for the safety of his soul. But never, from that first hour of rebellion, did the enfranchised mind of my father return to the old bondage of dogma. But as fortune, if not leisure, gave him opportunity, he purchased all the discoverable translations of the books of the ancient religions, in his typical desire to find out for himself the verities revealed by the great initiates, from whose number he in nowise excluded the founder of the Christian religion. Later he became a constant church-goer and was the adoration and despair of his successive pastors, for he generously supported

CHARLES B. FARWELL

MY MOTHER AND HER BROTHER
SOUTH WILLIAMSTOWN, CIRCA 1845

the church, while he aways refused to become what was called a "professing Christian."

Slowly, however, he arrived at what was to him an irreducible minimum of ethical truth, and this he compressed to the smallest compass of words. The Golden Rule was his guide, and never did an honest doubter more faithfully follow it. "If you have nothing pleasant to say about anybody," he always enjoined his children, "say nothing at all." Such was his invariable attitude toward gossip and unkind criticism and such were the principles which this political leader found practical, even in politics.

Titles to real estate and kindred cases occupied much of the county-court docket. In the growing city fortunes waited on real estate speculation. In this my father had already amassed a hundred thousand dollars, when the advent of his brother John gave a new turn to his business activities. A small firm of wholesale merchants, in what was called "dry goods," offered a partnership to this brother John, married to a former Miss Cooley, a sister of the Hartford merchant who, with a New York Wadsworth, represented this new organization. To enable his brother to enter the firm, the entire sum of my father's profits from real estate was unhesitatingly given to him, as the required sum for the partnership. Soon the firm became Cooley & Farwell, and then, although reluctantly, my father abandoned his career of land speculator and joined his brother in the business which, again renamed, was soon after called J. V. Farwell & Co. So passed in increasing business occupation the years until 1860 and the outbreak of the war of Rebellion. Then indeed came greatly increased opportunities of trade, whose advantages induced two other young men to enter the business, and these two were Marshall Field and Levi Leiter. If discordant elements of character had not broken the partnership of the Farwell brothers and their new associates, the history of Chicago's chief merchants would have been very different and far more fortunate for the Farwells. But John V., as the titular head of the firm was then colloquially named, had an obstinacy which collided with the same quality in the Jew Levi Leiter, and although no personal differences ever divided Charles Farwell and Marshall Field, the partnership was dissolved and Field & Leiter then set up for themselves. A great financial genius was Marshall Field, who died the possessor of hundreds of millions. His daughter became the wife of England's Admiral Beatty, and beautiful Mary Leiter became the Vicereine of India. So far, to the greatest prizes in the high places of the world, did the business beginnings in the mercantile house of Cooley & Wadsworth float their ultimate beneficiaries.

Marshall Field, as my mother remembered him in a little shop in Pittsfield, Massachusetts, when she was a schoolgirl in the early 'fifties, was a strikingly handsome, tall lad, with "dark hair, regular features, and cheeks as red as a rose." As I remember him, forty years later, the dark hair of youth had turned to snow, while the "regular features" had acquired great distinction and the eyes were authoritative and very reserved. This is my recollection of him, who for many years was Chicago's chief merchant and its richest. So he was, when last I dined with him and the son of Abraham Lincoln, in the Virginia Mountains, pleasantly talking and curiously regarding the daughter of his old partner.

With Marshall Field it was always business and more business, which brought enormous returns; but Charles Farwell was first the politician, and in the affairs of government at home and in Washington, in his relations with his political associates, in his influence as a leader of men, his nature found its principal expression and enjoyment. "A great game, politics," he was once heard to say, "to be competently played." Was he what was called a "machine politician?" That he was, surely, for "a machine there must be," as he often declared, "but an honest machine." A "stalwart Republican," he also was proud to be called, supporting generously party organizations.

These principles and methods he practiced as the local leader in Chicago and afterward in Congress. Soon after he became county clerk, he married, taking my mother, whom he met at the kindly home of an elderly friend, to a home of their own. Although New England by descent and upbringing, as was my father, my mother's assimilation of those traditions was far deeper and controlled the development of her character from youth to the last hour of her long life. Of my father it might be truly said that he "sought God, rather than the name of God." My mother, on the contrary, less independent in inquiry, had accepted Church doctrine as she had been taught it in the New England village where she passed her youth. That village, called South Williamstown, hard by the larger Williamstown and its college, preserved the earliest and strictest of Puritan observances. There, as in other Massachusetts towns, the church was the social as well as the religious center and its minister the ruler of the community. The church was called the "meeting house," and with typical Puritan self-approbation the people found there the chief amusement and interest of their lives. Thus, to my mother, religion was not only duty, but delight. In a letter to a sister, penned in her exquisite handwriting, she records her joy in an annual week of fasting and prayer, and declared that she had "never remembered a more delightful season of refreshment." Hand in hand with this religious ardor went a like enthusiasm for improving her mind. Before dawn, she insisted that her mother should awaken her, to study her Virgil by candlelight in the deep New England winters. The classics she studied in company with the daughters of President Hopkins of Williams College, and by these early influences, religious and educational, so deeply impressed on her youthful character, she was constantly guided in every act of her life.

The home of my mother in South Williamstown, as she often described it to her children, was a white house on a hill, just under Green Mountain, its pillared portico overlooking Green River. This was the home she left on her marriage, and sixty years later I saw it and delighted in the pure dignity of its architecture and its sturdy preservation. Built in the first years of the nineteenth century, it followed the beautiful lines of late Colonial houses, with a Georgian frieze under its eaves,

and classic pillars, while within was the excellent woodwork of the period—the pure line of staircase.

Here she lived with her parents, her brothers and two
younger sisters, with long intervals of school at Maple-
wood Seminary in Pittsfield, where later she was a
teacher. Then, going westward, she taught for a while
at Kinderhook, near New York, and shortly after went
to Chicago, where she met my father. After one of her
summer vacations to South Williamstown he followed
and married her, in the glory of a New England
autumn.

The first home of my parents in Chicago was one of
a row of brick houses, modest enough, but still ready to
receive, as part of the household, my father's parents,
his sister Louise, and sometimes also his brothers. And,
as if this family was not already quite overflowing, it
was increased during periods of necessity by my mother's sisters and their husbands. Among the numerous
letters preserved from those early days, letters of business and politics, there were many thanking my father,
"the best brother, the kindest of friends," for his ever-
ready assistance. He was, in truth, at that time the
leader and providence of all his family, as he was the
most generous of citizens. Too generous, as he later
came to believe, with the sad and embittering experience
of numberless unpaid loans and the inevitable enmity
of the debtors.

My mother's father was one of the countless New
England Smiths, but through her mother, Phoebe Angell, and her maternal grandmother, Lucinda Dexter,
she was connected with two well-known Colonial fam-

17

ilies of English origin. Although it is customary to assume that the Southern planters were descendants of younger sons of the English peerage and that New England was settled by farmers and shopkeepers, an examination of genealogical records shows that many New England families also descend directly from the English gentry. My mother's physical type was entirely Dexter and singularly similar to that of various members of this family whom I have known in Boston. Her nose, not quite straight, was aquiline. Her eyes were brown and luminous, her brows curved like a Lely portrait. Her hands were long and aristocratic and her skin very fair in her youth. She soon lost this fair complexion in the Western climate, but her melting brown eyes never lost their beauty. Her face developed great strength and seriousness, and in her old age she looked, curiously, but quite remarkably, like Washington. She inherited, also, from this dominant Dexter strain her graceful and fluent speech. I found the source of this in a paper among the family letters written for her by her great-grandfather, Nathan Dexter. As a revolutionary document, very expressive of the temper of the New England patriots, it has been considered interesting and is now included among the records of the Massachusetts Historical Society.

LANESBORO MASSACHUSETTS.　*July 29th. 1843.*

This short narrative is wrote at the request of my great granddaughter, Mary Eveline Smith. I am the sixth generation from Gregory Dexter who was born in Providence, Rhode Island, in 1643. I was born in Smith Town, Rhode Island, on July 23rd. 1759, and when at the age of sixteen I slung my pack

18

and shouldered my loaded gun in the defense of my dear country which was infested by a cruel and destructive inimy for seven years. When by the word of God and the Swoard of Washington they were made prisoners and drove back to their infernal den. I from the first have stood firm in the shoes of democracy and may God bless my dear country with peace and prosperity and happiness until time shall be no more.

The above lines wrote by the aged and trembling hand of Nathan Dexter in my eighty third year.

In a letter to one of her sisters my mother enjoined her to waste no moment in the task of improving her mind and of working for the salvation of her soul. No relaxation in these two objects was ever observed in my own life or conduct. She trained her children in the stern ways her own feet had trod and she was, doubtless, over-anxious often and suppressed for many years her delicious sense of humor, her wide and sympathetic charity, so deeply had the Puritan type of religious thought been stamped upon her character.

A number of her children died in their early youth, the first in infancy, and three others, the next eldest, from the dread diphtheria, then unchecked by the later discovery of its antitoxin. Mary and Henry, who died within a week of each other, were beautiful children, whose loss tragically altered my mother, leaving a deep well of agony in her heart, which was stirred at the least appeal to her emotions. Mary, with the luminous eyes of my mother, upward gazing, almost visionary, as pictured in the sweetest of early daguerreotypes, in her grandmother's arms, was a predestined angel in her docility and her intuitive comprehension of my mother's religious teachings. Henry was tall for his years, with

19

the noticeably fine head of my father and full of unful-
filled promise.

Slowly my mother recovered her courage. Edward,
the next boy, was then three years old, and Anna (myself) was the baby, and after the birth of Walter, a year
and a half later, she moved with these tiny children to
the far more commodious house which my father had
built in Chicago, and began a new chapter of life.

CHAPTER TWO

NO better indication of the profound and tenacious egoism of humanity exists than the exaggerated importance which all writers of "memoirs" ascribe to their infantile recollections. Realizing that I now take my place beside those egoists, I will try to evoke those first memories, or rather present the clear but unchangeable pictures which have survived from my infancy. No effort enlarges them or wakes one new detail; they are crystallized now—memories of memories—and thus have remained.

The very first of all, as seems quite proper and right to the daughter of my beloved father, is sweetly connected with him. He was firmly averse to any expression which was sentimental and rarely, if ever, uttered a caressing word, but with little children he could lavish the treasures of his heart in daily acts of loving gayety. I must have been a little less than three years old when this incident of his delight in his children echoed so keenly in his tiny daughter that it made on her consciousness an indelible impression. Our new house was built on the northwest corner of a long street running parallel with the Lake and called Wabash Avenue. It was made of pale cream-colored "Milwaukee" brick. It had a straight hall, opening from the entrance door, a parlor toward the north of the hall, and in front of the

21

parlor a wide window with a balcony surrounded by a stone railing. In front of the house, inclosed by a wrought-iron fence, was a green bit of lawn. This is the setting of my memory. Imagine, then, my father standing on the lawn, very tall and splendid, and with arms outstretched just beneath the balcony. Imagine also a round of babies, how many I cannot remember, running through the hall, into the parlor, through the open window, and with flying petticoats gaining the top of the stone balcony, to throw themselves, one after the other, into those waiting arms. Over and over again the circle was repeated, and as often, with laughter and cries of delight, each baby cast herself fearlessly into the air, to be caught by my father.

Next in my memory comes my birthday party when I had reached three years—another vibration of pleasure impressed on the tender wax of a child's mind. A group of children, gathering at the foot of the staircase, and I, the hostess, greeting them with pride and delight.

Then a blank for a year and a half, during which I know now that we had spent a winter in town and a summer at Lake Forest and had lingered there into the following winter. I had been ill, with the dread diphtheria, my brother Eddie far more seriously, and when, nursed by my aunt Nettie—my mother's youngest sister—I was returning with her to Lake Forest, she told me that my brother had died.

Four years cannot suffer deeply or long, but the choking sobs of my small pale self in the dim winter dusk of that hurrying train, the agony of that far-away little sister of this sad, remembering me, is still fresh with its first acquaintance with grief.

Broken already by the loss of Mary and Henry, my mother told me, later and often, and in words I have never forgotten, of the snow which drifted through the open window over the quiet little feet of one more of her beloved children. This sorrow darkened for a time my mother's joy in her always loved Lake Forest, where she spent many years. At this time we lived with a quaint Scotch couple, Sylvester Lind and his wife. Just opposite their modest white house, paralleling the pathway which wound eastward from the railroad station to the Lake, flowed a fresh little brook. "Lake Forest, Lake Forest," mused my mother, in the last summer of her life—"that name means all of happiness to me, and this gentle little stream, how I have loved it!" With these same accents I heard her repeat the initials of my father's name as she stood in all her bent and pale fragility by the stone which was to mark his grave.

A place of mystery and shadowed beauty in my child's memory was called Clark's Ravine. Through the thickly wooded plateau which, at Lake Forest, stands one hundred feet above Lake Michigan, many fissures called ravines wander, each with its silver stream, to open wide mouths to the Lake. Clark's Ravine—a long summer walk from Sylvester Lind's cottage, was deeply set with immemorial evergreens. One great cedar, falling across the stream, had made a bridge over which my mother used to lead me to the fragrant softness of moss and fallen drifts of leaves— a cool couch beneath the green. There she read to me.

What was the book? *Line upon Line—Precept upon Precept*—a book of sweet old platitudes, bringing tears and avowals dear to her ears. Then, after the reading, docile child and happy mother, hand in hand, would wander through the summer twilight back to Sylvester's.

The next scene, well remembered, was in still another house in Chicago, which faced the Lake directly, on Michigan Avenue. I can recall my mother sitting in a back room of this house, called the nursery, with several women—her sister, probably, an old friend of the family, and the nurse. Then in the early morning, as I was called into the room, I saw, not my mother, but two pink-faced mites, each clad in a still pinker garment, held up to my astonished eyes. Thus I was introduced to my new brother and sister. To whom first did I fly to announce the wonderful news? Whom but my father? "Oh, papa, do listen," I can hear myself say, as I stood with head just reaching the top of the bureau, where, after a sleepless night, he was repairing his toilet, "There are two—yes—two new babies. Did you know it?"

Even now I get the little shock that glance of gentle humor gave me—the idea that in some way he already knew about it.

For a few years only the Michigan Avenue house was our abode. The penetrating moisture from the Lake made my throat very delicate, and the memory of many little illnesses, less dangerous than diphtheria, remain in my mind. The time when I was punished for lying, and another, to me deeply disgraceful incident when I revealed to a popular playmate the intention of my little group of comrades to give her a surprise party, belong to this eight-year-old period and were ineffaceably marked upon my character.

I can bring up the picture of my despised little self, most unbecomingly dressed in the large plaids which our German dressmaker, Lizzie Wagner, fashioned for us (even now I can see her patient stolid face), with my hair parted from my forehead and braided in two cruelly tight tails adorned with large bows of green ribbon. Thus was my head, too large for a child, presented to the view of my comrades. It has been asserted by various members of my family that my mother's study of Josephus during the months antedating my birth had filled this large head with historical preoccupations. Whatever religious or historical tastes might have been realized from those maternal influences— and they have not been important—the attention to the harmonious exterior of her daughter did not absorb my mother. Sometimes, indeed, my usually imprisoned hair was frizzed, to still further increase the effect of my cranial development, and in a cherry overdress, with a tucked muslin petticoat, I was sent, with much straining of my mother's principles, to dancing school. Few indeed are those memories of Chicago, for our anxious mother soon persuaded our father to build in Lake Forest our permanent home.

I have naturally no recollection of the birth of my brother Walter, scarcely more than a year younger than I, nor, strangely, do I remember that of my sister Grace, which followed some five years later. But when we moved to our home in the country there were then living five of my mother's nine children—myself, Anna, the eldest; Walter; Grace; and the twins, Rose and Robert. Grace was a chubby blond baby of three, dimpled and lovely. Walter, blue-eyed and blond also. Anna, very serious and motherly with her juniors, and the twins, who were quite entrancing in their infantile beauty. This was the little family which filled the new home with laughter and childish voices, that house which was to be our home for full fifty years.

The house was built on a terrace, on a plot of land very near the bluff of Lake Michigan. It was large and very comfortable and of the prevailing style of architecture of the period, whose date, 1870, was set over the entrance door. A distinct accentuation of the Victorian order was introduced, however, by the patient labor of my father's protégé, the German Hillexe, who laid down inlaid floors, built elaborate architraves over the doorways, and made the library a marked example of carved and inlaid woodwork. Toward the south, in a curved extension, was a conservatory which was later transformed into a picture gallery, surrounded by inlaid cabinets to hold my father's collection of illustrated books and engravings. During the years of my father's service in Washington as a member of Congress, he bought many pictures of a dealer called Barlow, into whose hands had fallen the works of art possessed by Southern families lately impoverished by the Civil War. For prices which would now be considered laughably small my father purchased pictures by Lawrence, David Wilson, Salvator Rosa, Vernet, and others, which have been pronounced to be authentic by expert opinions. The parlor in our house, as it was originally furnished, had a carpet with roses and red damask curtains. A bay window opened out toward the lawn, and windows toward the east on a porch, where for many happy years we sat together, looking out on the changing hues of the Lake. Although years have passed by, and fire has destroyed it, still in my thoughts and my dreams it is home. Here we lived "all the year round," and soon after our removal to the country, Uncle John, with his three boys and two daughters, built his house nearly opposite. Lake Forest had a very definite character, not only for the beauty of its situation, near and just over the waters of Michigan, but also for its unusual plan. Called first "Lake" from its situation, its deep and luxurious woods added "Forest," and the landscape artist of reputation, who had been employed by the founders of the village, did not follow the usual rectilinear plan for villages, but laid out the roads in curves which wound among the ravines from the sunset plains toward the west to the overlooking bluff of the Lake.

A school for girls and another for boys were already established when we came to live in Lake Forest. These advantages had induced a group of members of a Chicago church to settle in this suburb, and their very strict Puritanical beliefs and customs gave the character of early New England to the community. They were all men of business and all "took" the eight o'clock train for Chicago. Mr. Holt and Mr. Ward and Mr. Skinner, whose houses were grouped about the little white church near the center of the village, were "elders," and the first two not only eloquent at the Wednesday-evening prayer meetings, but very strict in their supervision of the young people of the town. Although a member of the church at the ripe age of ten, I was reported to the council of elders for inattention at prayer by the stern Mr. Ward, but could never understand why his own eyes should be open to observe my reprehensible conduct. Mr. Holt was still sterner, advising even my mother, when she had praised the saintliness of one of her friends, to "try to be like her."

Missionary ardor, of which my mother, for twenty-five years the treasurer of the Presbyterian Board of Foreign Missions, was a notable exponent, burned high in Lake Forest. At the home of Mrs. Rhea, a returned missionary, I joined in a little girls' prayer meeting, on my knees and in fright, adding my supplications to those of my comrades. However, there were some distractions from these so seriously directed occupations of the Lake Forest maidens, due, it must be confessed, to the presence of the boys' academy in those Puritan groves. Not unwillingly did I hie me, through the deep winter snow, in a pink knitted hood, to the prayer meetings, for after the service was there not always a group of "academy boys" awaiting my appearance, and the invariable invitation, from almost always just the right boy, "Miss Farwell, may I see you home?" And then the walk home over the scarce trodden snow, under moonlight or starlight, and the shy words of lingering good-by at the gate, repeated—remembered, when prayers of the graybeards were quickly forgotten. So passed the years of my "teens," favored enough for this village maiden, with pony and phaeton in which she drove this boy or another, when the snows had yielded to green-leaved summer in those woods of magical youth. Did she not have, also, a boat on the miniature lake at her own home, "Fairlawn," when, rowing or moored by the moonlit willows, she could sing songs to her sweethearts? Innocent youth, innocent dreams, and as happy as innocent. The day's work during the school terms was quite rigidly marked. Seven-o'clock breakfast, with sometimes white-fish fresh from the Lake, was followed by family "devotions," when I would play hymns on the piano in the sitting room, after my mother's Bible-reading and prayer. Then a run "across lots," over fences, and down the ravines to the girls' seminary, where, until noon, I attended my classes. The afternoon for play and the evening for study made up the day's program, from September to July, when idle months intervened until not only the seminary, but the academy, opened again with new recruits of playmates and friends.

Our religious instruction at home was a mixture of my mother's careful teaching, purely evangelical, and my father's ethical maxims, which, simple and often repeated, were fixed in our minds. My early years were greatly tormented by certain church doctrines. I still remember my struggle with the rule that we should love our enemies. Enemies of my own being non-existent, the problem I faced was to love those of my father. There was a dire enemy of that idol of my childhood, a political foe, whose wicked name and intentions had assumed formidable proportions. Only by imagining the enemy in the throes of illness and death could I conjure up enough pity to meet the Bible requirements, when in triumph I announced to my astonished mother that I loved the adversary. But, as I grew older, eternal punishment which would surely engulf all who were not "Christians" became a real and persistent terror. My father, as I was told, was not a real 'Christian," as he had not declared his faith, and of no church was he a member. The religion which condemned him to eternal damnation was not my religion. So did the *argumentum ad hominem* wave a forbidding sword before the faith of my father's child and set her young thoughts in the way he had followed. Not until the study of the New Testament in Greek, with the discovery that the word "unending" was never used in the original to designate the punishment of unbelievers, was the terror of my father's damnation lifted from my childhood. Well I remember my triumphant announcement of this liberating discovery to my uncle John, the evangelist, the Bible student. "Anna," he sternly declared, "you must believe in eternal damnation; the Bible teaches it. You will be punished if you refuse to believe."

"But, uncle, the Greek word is not eternal," I insisted.

"I thank my Heavenly Father," he answered, "that I do not base my theology on a Greek word."

"And I, dear uncle," was my probably very irritating reply, "am thankful that I need not base mine on a translation."

There was much of warm affection for his young

LAKE OF FAIR LAWN, LAKE FOREST

THE FARWELL HOME, LAKE FOREST

nephews and nieces in this sturdy uncle, who used to sing hymns to them as they gathered in a group, with his own children, around his porch chair, after Sunday-morning service in those long-ago summers. John V., his eldest son, named after his father, inheriting the Farwell brain and capacity, had also much of his mother's Eastern conservatism. Although conservative, Mrs. J. V. Farwell was the most loving mother to her very happy family and lived long to devote herself to that happiness. Frank was the next oldest, very near my own age, and a loving friend through all the years which have followed since that time of our youthful companionship. Blue-eyed and frank as his name, he was loved at college by all who knew him. Arthur, the third boy, with regular features, unlike the Farwells, is all Cooley, while Fannie, the idolized daughter, with pretty features and a beautiful brow, was and is a character of remarkable fidelity and sweetness. Another daughter, elder than all, the child of my uncle's first brief marriage, had great beauty and more than a hint of literary and dramatic ability, shown in essays and amateur plays. She soon married and took up her abode in a house not far from her father. Her sons, one a minister, another showing great promise of abilities as a naturalist, but unfortunately cut off in his youth, and two others successful in business, inherited the Farwell ability.

In those years from 1870 to 1880 we, the children of Charles, made almost one family with John's children, just over the way. Rose and Robert were too little to join in our play and soon Robert was tragically killed by the fall of a dead branch of a tree; so was the exquisite duo of Rose and her twin untimely cut short, and thus sorrow, the only one for over twenty-five years, interrupted the joy of our childhood and youth. At school, at church, at play, in our lovely Lake Forest, those early years passed peacefully by.

I cannot believe, as I look back on those so distant years, that my adoring love for my father was quite unreturned. My accustomed seat was his knee and the playful tenderness of his comradeship was the background of my life. His interests, as far as I could comprehend them, his political fortunes, and his religious beliefs, were my constant preoccupations. At last, after nearly twenty years of leadership in Chicago, he was elected a member of Congress, and although I was at school, my father, unwilling to leave me behind, took me with him to Washington.

CHAPTER THREE

I WAS still a short-skirted child when I first saw the capital. We lived, during that winter of my father's first term of Congress, in a small hotel on H Street, conducted by a certain very aimable Mrs. Rines, where a number of official people combined to make an agreeable and intimate household. Mr. Boutwell from Massachusetts, then Secretary of the Treasury, and his wife were there in that winter of 1871-72. Various members of Congress also belonged to this household, among them Mr. Wheeler, afterward Vice-President with Hayes. The friendship which they showed for the new representative from Chicago and his wife was extended to the little girl I was then, as many singularly charming letters from Mr. Wheeler, preserved among my treasures, quite touchingly prove.

In Washington, as at home, I was my father's constant comrade. How proudly fond he was of his children had no more striking expression than his habit of taking me with him to the Capitol. Hand-in-hand with him I would slip past the indulgent sergeant-at-arms who stood at the door of the House of Representatives; then, seated as usual on my father's knee, I would watch the proceedings.

A few impressions, clear as flashlight pictures, I have retained since that time when the House of Representa-

33

tives was my school and my playground. First is the picture of the Hall itself, crowded with faces, murmurous with voices, as the business of state was conducted. Blaine the magnetic, "the plumed knight of his party," was the Speaker. With a wide, rapid gesture he would count the votes in a rising ballot. It was quite impossible that the lightning calculation of his gavel should accurately report such a ballot, but such was his custom except in close divisions of the opposing parties. In later years I often met Mr. Blaine and recognized that the dash and spectacular brilliancy of his career were the expression of a personality rarely surpassed in ability and impetuous vitality. His appearance was also entirely in harmony with his character. His dark eyes, now blazing, now dreaming, illumined a commanding physiognomy. His manner with men and women was at once chivalrous and imperious, and his speech rapid and shot through with disconcerting shafts of wit and authoritative opinion. Too emotional for the political arena, too partisan, and sometimes too hasty in action, he narrowly failed in his presidential campaigns to achieve the reward of his great ambition. As I saw him first, when he was Speaker, he was in the first strength of his youth, and the impression of power, even of delight, in his control of the House of Representatives remains clearly in my memory. Sometimes my friend Mr. Wheeler was asked to take the Speaker's chair, and his serene and quiet demeanor, strongly in contrast with Blaine's dramatic attitude, is another of the pictures in the little girl's gallery. Years later I sat beside Mr. Blaine at dinner in the last month of his life. The sick lion was silent, and his dark eyes were despairing as I saw them fixed on his own pallid hand. There was death in that hand and I saw that he knew it. This was my last meeting with him whom I had seen so full of strength and promise. A silent exchange of impressions dramatic and unforgettable.

Another recollection of that winter of 1872 has something of historical interest. It was the scene of an impeachment, rare in the history of our government, and this celebrated case was called the affair of the "Crédit Mobilier." Oakes Ames and James Brooks, both members of Congress, were to be judged at its bar. The work of these men in the great project which was destined to bind the two oceans with railroads and give an enormous impetus to our country's development has had its tardy recognition, with the further conclusion that Ames at least was strangely but actually ignorant of the moral turpitude of his connection as a member of Congress with a project to be supported by government subsidies. On the day of the trial Brooks had been assigned to my father's seat, and my father, holding me on his knee, was only a few feet away. Seeing my small self from the galleries, which were crowded to danger, the demand of the many women spectators to be given seats on the floor of the Chamber was acceded to for this time, and this time only. I remember no words which were spoken on this tragically famous occasion, but if I were a painter I could now reproduce the faces of the men who were publicly condemned for dishonesty by this government court. With his head in his

35

hand, Brooks sat so near me! I watched him, struck with pity and terror, as the tears rained down his cheeks. It was death that I saw in that face, the death of dishonor—he lived only three weeks after his condemnation. Oakes Ames, as he rose to receive his conviction, is equally clear in my memory. A tall oak of a man, the color of health was still in his face, but he was weeping as openly as his companion, and he also succumbed under the mortal blow of this public disgrace. Fifty years of our history have passed in the march of our country to its almost fabulous prosperity. I wonder how many of those whose great fortunes have followed in the way these fallen pioneers had opened recall how they fell.

I spent, at this period, only that one winter with my parents in Washington, and Lake Forest absorbed me again with its lessons and play. I spent five years at the seminary, and then my mother began to dream of giving me that "higher education" which, since her classical studies with Mark Hopkins's daughters, she believed all girls should receive. But to send me away she was too anxiously unwilling, she who had lost so many of her idolized children, so it came about that after long and persistent persuasion my father initiated the project of adding a coeducational collegiate department (just for this daughter) to the already established boys and girls preparatory schools. It was he who built the first college hall in the park near the boys' academy, but while it was in process of construction professors and students assembled for recitation, first in an old hotel near the Lake and next in a disused building in the little park near the station. Professors, and very excellent ones, were lured by good salaries and the hope of founding a new institution of learning in the prosperous West. Morris, later of Yale, became one of the best Latinists of the country, and Hewitt, professor of Greek and very dearly beloved, was most successful in the new college, and later was professor and sometimes acting president of Williams College. Students were far more difficult to find. Nothing daunted, my mother directed my cousin, Charles Ward, just emerged from a Chicago high school and himself a prospective freshman in the new institution, to hunt out poor and ambitious comrades who would accept an education paid for by my father. My cousin's efforts produced two students, the pallid and poetic Eben Wells and a brilliant girl, called Josephine White, who was destined to pursue the whole course at my side.

The first time I saw this friend of my youth was at a high-school Commencement as she stood on the platform to deliver her graduating oration, a rhymed essay on "Woman's Rights." Slight and straight, with the dark eyes of her French Canadian birth, she stood in her youthful enthusiasm, her deep voice defiant with courage and idealism. For four years without failure we attended the selfsame classes, and at the end of those years, out to four decimal points, our marks were the same. Such a result, strange in itself, could only mean diligent study. Our professors were engaged in establishing a record for scholarship and their requirements were strict. Greek and Latin, carried through many classic authors, higher mathematics, logic and psychology, science, confined to a minute memorizing of Ganot's *Physics,* with a few experiments in chemistry, limited history and as limited political economy, were taught us, but habits of study and concentration were gained in those strenuous years. Little time was left for what was called recreation. There was no college life, for there were not enough pupils to compose one, and the sum of my college experience amounted to a rigid tutoring in my own home.

The eloquence of my college mate, Josephine White, was destined for a famous opportunity when, as the wife of the well-known engineer, Lindon Bates, she spoke from many platforms in aid of our first efforts for Belgium and in the preparedness campaign before we entered the war.

During these studious years in Lake Forest I saw almost nothing of Chicago. One appearance I made in my sixteenth year, when my father took me to a reception at the Chicago Club given in honor of General Grant, who had just returned from his European tour. In a pretty dress of flowered brocade with a blue-satin bodice and overdress, I, too early, met a certain blue-eyed Englishman, far too old for my girlhood fancy. He is dead these many years, as are all of the others I saw in this first glimpse of the world. He followed my growth and attended the graduation exercises when I finished my "college course." His photograph has disappeared in the flotsam of life, but a bit of that old brocade of my sixteenth year makes the opera bag I use now.

Another Chicago appearance was on January 1 of

my eighteenth year, when I assisted Mrs. Franklin
Mac Veagh in her New-year's Day reception. Not only
in Chicago, but all over our country it was the custom
for all hostesses on New-year's Day to open their doors
to their masculine friends, who, imbibing the punch
which was offered them, called from house to house, in
an increasing merriment, from early morning until
nightfall. Mrs. Franklin Mac Veagh was very charming in those early days, a blond and aimable young
matron, the very type of a "merry wife." Franklin
Mac Veagh, like his brother Wayne, was engaged in the
very democratic occupation of a wholesale grocer.
He was, however, really distinguished, if this word
represents impeccable standards of character, high
loyalty in personal relationships, as high a sense of civic
responsibility, and a cultivated mind. He was, in those
days, exceedingly charming in appearance, with a delicately modeled face of great intelligence. Later he
became Secretary of the Treasury and the house he built
in Washington was filled, like that in Chicago, with
books and pictures and Chinese porcelains, set, according to Mrs. Mac Veagh's very colorful taste, among
vistas of gold-lacquered rooms opening through tapestried corridors into the fountain-cooled greenness of
conservatories. These kind friends of my girlhood
were exceedingly discriminating and very anxious to
recognize any indication of promise in the younger generation. Mrs. Mac Veagh was more keenly acquisitive
of any new accomplishment or knowledge, more enthusiastic, and more courageous than anyone I have
ever known. Mr. Mac Veagh had—and still has—a sen-

sitive philosophical turn of mind which I have always found exceedingly sympathetic and helpful. In my eighteenth year the problems I discussed with him were on a wholly imaginative and speculative basis, and our conversations only brief interludes in my absorbing and sometimes exhausting studies in college. I could almost weep over an eighteenth year spent in such close application to my lessons that only one hour was left for a walk at the close of the day. All my early academy boy playmates had departed to Eastern colleges and afforded me no more of the youthful distractions of summer walks and drives or of sleighing by moonlight. The vacations, also in Lake Forest, before there was golf or auction bridge, were quiet enough. But at last the four years of my college course were over, and on Commencement day, in the crowded church, before the college president, the professors, and all the students and residents of the town, I delivered, clad appropriately in white muslin, the valedictory oration. This oration, as I reread it, was an unsurpassed collection of hopeful platitudes, but the honor of its delivery, thus awarded to me, gave, at least to my parents, one proud summer day.

A little worn down by the close application to my studies, and older in appearance than my years, I began to look out upon life. Just then the historically famous Republican convention for the nomination of President had assembled in Chicago in the month of June, 1880. With my father, I had a place on the platform. The "tickets" prepared by the two principal candidates and their supporters were fiercely contested. General

Grant, with General Logan as probable candidate for Vice-President, were pertinaciously supported by a large faction against James G. Blaine. Thus supported, in spite of the prejudice against the "third term" the twice-elected President Grant would have received the nomination but for my father's influence in his section of northern Illinois. A "bolt" from the Cook County convention, ordered by Logan, of the minority favoring Grant and himself, made a majority in the state convention at Springfield to send the "solid" Illinois delegation to the Chicago convention in favor of the Grant ticket. My father's influence in Cook County was too strongly adverse to this illegal proceeding and the "bolt" was ineffectual; the minority delegates were thrown out at Springfield, the Illinois vote was divided and so remained in spite of the frenzied efforts of Grant's old guard, who needed just that solid vote for nomination. Garfield's eloquent speech against what was called the "unit rule," which would have disfranchised the anti-Grant districts, made this issue the most important in the convention. Published protests of the ignored districts, dictated by my father, and a mass meeting in Chicago itself, made the basis of Garfield's argument, the principles of which, as he declared, were of greater moment in a free country than the nomination of any candidate. From the platform, the scene was very exciting to my young observation. Robert Ingersoll sat near my father and me, commenting sarcastically upon the bombastic reiteration of Roscoe Conkling, as with a shaking of his "Hyperion" curls he announced that the "imperial State of New York had

41

the honor of casting its vote for General Ulysses S. Grant." I heard also the renowned query of Flanigan of Texas, "What are we here for? To the victors belong the spoils," delivered in a falsetto shout which still rings in my ears. Flanigan was bearded and frenetic, with yellow coat tails waving, speaking his political truth to the breezes. Then, of course, I remember the rising excitement of the thickly massed spectators in the galleries, who were, in the last stage of the battle, the real nominating members of this famous convention. Their enthusiasm at Garfield's speech swept the hall, and before anyone knew exactly how it happened all the rival groups melted together and Garfield found himself the nominee of the convention.

After this interesting experience I spent a summer in Lake Forest, and in the autumn went for a "finishing course" to Mrs. Sylvanus Read's school in New York City as a "parlor boarder." I found no interest in the parlor of this girls' school and betook myself daily to the studio of Wyatt Eaton, a follower of the then dominant Barbizon School, where I studied drawing.

Mrs. Read's eldest daughter, whose beautiful portrait by Eaton is perhaps the best work of this too little known painter, suggested that I should study with him. The complete ascendency of the Barbizon influence upon both Mr. Eaton and Miss Read was proved by Eaton's marriage to a French peasant woman, whom he had known while studying in France, and Miss Read's marriage to the son of Jean François Millet. The first and only sonnet I ever composed was about Millet, for I also came under this influence. This sonnet, together

MRS. REGINALD DE KOVEN
NEW YORK, 1880

with the portrait of myself painted by Eaton during the brief three months' study with him, are reminders of a very interesting interlude between college and the wider but less significant life of the world I was destined to enter. Mr. Eaton took a very encouraging view of my capabilities as a student. I was first set to drawing from the cast. "Did you do this yourself?" he asked me one day as he looked at one of my drawings. "I was afraid that some one had helped you. In a few weeks you can use colors and begin to do portraits." I was so encouraged by this unexpected praise, so thrilled by the stimulating atmosphere of the studio, that if it had not been for my mother's refusal I would willingly have continued these studies. His portrait of me shows a face full of dreams, but that of becoming a painter was not to be fulfilled. But as I have passed the corner of 4th Avenue and 14th Street and the German Bank building in which was Mr. Eaton's studio, I have often wondered if it was really myself who there dreamed and worked and aspired in that far-away youth.

One incident of my stay at Mrs. Read's school was memorable. A certain Mrs. Botta, a poetess herself, had a "literary house" in New York, and it had been reported to my mother that she sometimes took young ladies under her wing. While living under her roof the lovely Consuelo Yznaga had been successfully introduced to New York in spite of Mrs. Botta's entirely literary associations. Mrs. Botta was asked through a friend to receive me also, but she no longer desired to assume the task so remarkably accomplished with the future Duchess of Manchester, and I was therefore sent

43

to Mrs. Read's school. But Mrs. Botta one day remembered the rejected candidate for her valuable instructions and invited me to luncheon. It was the day in November which happened to be my birthday, and on this, to me, intensely thrilling occasion, I had my first opportunity of meeting people of literary distinction. Oliver Wendell Holmes was there and Moncure Conway. From the end of the table I drank in every one of their words. The subject of their conversation was their membership in a lately established "Rabelais Club," which they discussed with great pride and interest. In my ramblings in my father's library, during the long summer vacations, in the days when there was no golf and no bridge, I had discovered Renan's "Life of Christ," the reading of which had early made a basis for a form of religious belief very similar to that of my father. I had also found at the age of fifteen Boccaccio's *Decameron,* but had not come upon Rabelais. Therefore, on a visit to my father at Washington, during that winter, I proceeded to the Congressional Library and demanded of my father's astonished old friend, Mr. Spofford, the librarian, the works of the great French master of pornographic prose. I remember the scrutinizing glance which Mr. Spofford bent upon me from his desk and my bewilderment at the enthusiasm of Dr. Holmes and Mr. Conway over the author of a thin book on law, which was the sole portion of Rabelais' works furnished by my father's friend to his inquiring young daughter. What the life of a physician and the wit and wisdom of a sage and philosopher had to say on the face of Dr. Holmes was a clear map to my young and intensely aroused observation. Humor was drawn in every little line and whimsical curve of his mouth. Enthusiasm, imagination, and kindness shone in his still beautiful eyes.

I do not recall that he spoke at all with his young observer, but after luncheon a number of the guests, including Mr. Conway and myself, visited the Metropolitan Museum. Hand in hand with Mr. Conway I followed Mr. Cesnola, then the curator, as he conducted us among his favorite pictures and stopped to show us the new acquisitions. I well remember his pause before a vitrine containing a row of terra-cotta masks from Central America and his comments upon their Chinese character. This was my first introduction to the unsolved problem of the origin of the races of the South American continent.

The recollection of Dr. Holmes's face is one of the indelible impressions of my youth and has often been recalled as, in succeeding years, I have observed the impress of character upon faces. In Paris, many years later, I went with Madame Jusserand's sister to a meeting of the "Académie des Sciences Morales et Politiques" and looked down from a high seat in the gallery of the church in which the meeting took place, upon a collection of scientists and sociologists whose faces, old, deeply modeled, and white as carved ivory, were *chefs d'œuvre* of the inner artificer which molds the material envelope into its own likeness. Thus the lesson of Dr. Holmes's face was repeated, and, as I have also observed the universal recognition of all good and kindly faces, of no matter what clime or nation, it has seemed to me a clear indication that goodness and kindness are and should be supreme and victorious. A Turkish imam, with a face of saintliness and eyes of pure benignity, illustrated the same deeply suggestive truth as I watched him teaching a group of crouching women in a mosque in Constantinople.

To Dr. Holmes I owe, also, the first hint that this same inner artificer, this ego, is undying and unaging. Old age is an illusion of youth and this illusion was as fully mine as another's, so that I scarcely understood the significance of the following little conversation between Dr. Holmes and Julia Ward Howe's daughter, Maud, when she repeated it to me. Emerging from her mother's house in Beacon Street, on a morning of blue sky and sunlight, she encountered Dr. Holmes, who asked for news of her mother.

"She is perfectly well," replied her daughter, "and younger than I am."

"Of course she should be," replied Dr. Holmes. "Her day's work is done. She can play. I thought when I was nineteen that this blue sky would be dim to me when I grew old. It is not. It gives me the same rapture as when I was young. Don't forget what I have told you, my dear."

The memory of the luncheon at Mrs. Botta's has always been a very happy one. It was indeed a "red letter day," and perhaps indicative of my own powers of perception and enjoyment, which have contributed the greatest pleasures in a life of many phases and places.

After my visit to Washington I spent a few weeks

at a hotel in Chicago, as my parents, at that time, had no house in the city.

The winter was already far advanced, but my mother somewhat summarily introduced me to society at a dinner at this hotel. There were still balls, however, at dancing halls and in private houses, and these I attended, escorted, as was the custom, by one or other of the men with whom I was acquainted. Many of these were English or Canadian, attractive, and successfully taking their part in the growing prosperity of the city. There were also occasional performances of opera, and on one memorable evening, before the streets were clear of the heavy winter snowfall, I went in a two-seated sleigh with a friend to hear Patti. Chaperons were not necessary in Chicago in those days, however much they were required in diplomatic Washington. After this experimental winter between a New York studio and a Chicago début my mother persuaded my father to abandon, for a few months, the political fray and take the family to Europe.

We crossed on the *Bothnia* and were duly seasick on that antiquated old steamer, but finally enjoyed ourselves immensely on the clear sunny voyage, finding enlivening company in a group of college boys bound for a rowing trip on the rivers of Europe. With them we older children sang college songs under the moonlight, and, behind the wheelhouse, my own singing of Scotch ballads brought applause from Andrew Carnegie, then for the first time returning to Scotland in company with his mother, a fierce old Scotch peasant and the most authoritative parent I ever encountered. Mr. Carnegie

invited me to join a company of his Pittsburgh associates
on a coaching trip through Scotland, but I did not wish
to be separated from my family and we left the *Bothnia*
to land in Ireland. At Blarney Castle my father held
my pretty little sister Rose head downward so that she
might kiss the celebrated stone, a salutation whose magic
she did not fail to wield during all the years of her lovely
youth. At the Lakes of Killarney my singing of Irish
songs brought the same applause from the boatmen as
I had received from Mr. Carnegie. "Innocents abroad"
we doubtless were, my sisters, my young brother, and I,
but we were very happy and enjoyed every moment. A
lightning trip was ours as, quite unfatigued by long
days of travel, we sped through the countries of Europe,
visiting, not only the principal cities and sights of Great
Britain, but of Germany, France, Austria, Switzerland,
and Holland. In a large open barouche, containing
father, mother, and four children, we would drive from
our hotels to visit the sights noted by our guide books.
In July, one broiling hot day, such a barouche drove
up to the Cologne Cathedral, only to find that our
vehicle was stopped by a similar one at the door. But
this was quite empty except for a very fat coachman,
sound asleep on his box in the sun. Leaning out of the
carriage, my father perceived a weary old man, in his
shirt sleeves, with a gray chin beard and with face submerged in his hands, seated on the steps of the cathedral.
"Why, there's my old friend Lancaster!" my father exclaimed. "I haven't seen him in thirty years! . . . Lancaster, old man, what's the matter?" he asked, jumping
out of the carriage and slapping his friend on the back.

By this time I had followed and heard the reply. "Why, Charlie,"he drawled,"I saw this d—— church yesterday, but" (with a thumb pointing at the coachman) "I can't make him understand and he won't take me away." Thirty years had not dimmed the affectionate remembrance of this old Springfield friend, nor my father's political memory for faces. To the end of his eighty years he was "Charlie" to his contemporaries. Our last stop was Paris, where in a vast trunk my trousseau, not for marriage, but for my first winter in Washington, was collected from Worth's.

CHAPTER FOUR

O N our return to America the younger children were
established in their several schools and I went to
Washington with my parents in December, 1881. The
point de depart for this new experience was the Arlington Hotel. Our apartments consisted of two bedrooms,
mine a tiny one at the end of a hall, and a large parlor.
This had blue-satin furniture and a carpet blazing with
roses, a marble-topped table and a rosewood "what-
not," innocent of ornaments except a large Chinese
plate, bought by myself, to hold visiting cards. Young,
with a memory so keen that for years I could recall
every word of my conversations with the distinguished
people I was so fortunate to meet, that winter was one
of intensest delight. Not at first, for my home-loving,
serious-minded mother had planned no social "campaign" for her daughter. Three solitary weeks passed
in the strange city, known only before to the little girl
of the earlier time when Mrs. Logan, wife of the Illinois
Senator, was minded, providentially, to invite my
mother and me to a church "sociable." Thither I went,
and there met two army officers; one of them hailed
from Chicago and had heard of Mr. Farwell. No sooner
introduced to me, Lieutenant Cotton asked me to dance
the cotillion at the next Bachelors' Ball, and his comrade, named Hines, asked me for the following one. To

50

the first I went clad in a green embroidered muslin with a guimpe up to my ears.

Not one person asked me to dance except my very discouraged partner. But my eyes had not been idle and I had seen that guimpes were distinctly unnecessary. Two weeks later, clad in a triumphant Worth ball dress of white tulle and snowballs (alas for the snows of those yester years!) and with my young shoulders happily free from all incumbrances, I found myself as the partner of Lieutenant Hines, who was leader of the cotillion, at the head of a long row of couples, in the very center of the ballroom. And I saw also a group of young men gathered together and all very markedly looking at me. Fresh from Lake Forest with its neighborhood prayer-meetings, I wonder why I should have assumed from their apparent consultation that they did not regard my partner with favor sufficient to ask him to introduce them to me. I knew in that ballroom just one person other than my partner, and this was Robert Lincoln, then Secretary of War, son of Abraham Lincoln, and a Chicago friend of my father. No sooner was I returned to my seat than I left it to seek Mr. Lincoln.

"Will you dance with me, please, Mr. Lincoln?" I asked, I suppose somewhat shyly.

"Why, my child," he replied, "I don't know how to dance! I know nothing about it."

"Never mind, dear Mr. Lincoln. I have a particular reason. Please, just once round the room."

Then with a high polka step, droll enough in my memory, he did take a half-turn and stopped, embarrassed and laughing. It was enough and my conclusion

51

was quickly seen to be right, for, with one rush, like a football team, my group of dancers were at his side and I was there and then introduced to Washington.

Then began the gayest and pleasantest time of all my life. Many more balls I attended, sometimes accompanied by my father, he who hated such functions and who had never permitted my mother to uncover her beautiful shoulders. The group of dancers, most of them army and navy officers, became my constant adherents at the houses which were open during the two winters of my Washington experience. A most agreeable, almost eighteenth-century custom prevailed during this time, when the hostesses of prominence received on their selected evenings a number of permanently invited guests. This number, hardly more than a hundred, included the Supreme Court judges, Cabinet Ministers, the Diplomatic Corps, ambassadors and secretaries, the prominent Senators, fewer members of Congress, the important Washington residents, and the President himself. Among those hostesses was Mrs. Frelinghuysen, wife of the Secretary of State, with her three daughters, Miss Mathilda, Miss Lucy, and Mrs. John Davis. Miss Mathilda was tall, like her sisters, with a fleckless white skin and features of greatest distinction. Mrs. Davis, the youngest, was a *charmeuse,* then as always, darkly beautiful, with a wit which made her famous, while Miss Lucy, the real and able conductor of the most representative house in the capital, had the aquiline features of her family and a rare and real cultivation. To this house my father one evening conducted me, and there I was introduced to President Arthur.

Mrs. James G. Blaine was another of the hostesses, in her new house on the hill, and there she and her husband and the children—three sons and three daughters—were all to be seen. At more intimate times, at their table, I listened to their rapid-fire talk of politics and family raillery. No one who had ever heard this family talk, pointed and led by Blaine himself and the remarkable woman who was his adoring wife, and the no less adoring mother of the gifted children, could ever forget it. Gail Hamilton, their cousin, was one of the family, and her literary talent and extraordinarily keen and trenchant comments on life and people left an indelible impression upon me, as they did on all her hearers. Walker and Emmons, the eldest two sons, were most unhappily cut off in early manhood. Walker had every capacity of mind with real political knowledge and promise, never, alas! to be exercised. Emmons, studious and steadfast in character, if less brilliant than Walker, was a sacrifice to the heat and excitement of a presidential convention, when he neglected a threatened illness to aid his father's never to be realized ambitions. One daughter, Alice, died soon after marriage, and the two surviving daughters, Mrs. Damrosch and Mrs. Beale, still represent the standards and capacities of their remarkable parents. Mrs. Blaine's published letters to her children record a full and interesting existence and show how romantic love for husband and children can glorify life. High-tempered, intellectually vivid, and intensely partisan, she is very clear in my memory, with her strongly marked features, her very decided voice, and her no less decided opinions.

I first saw Walter Damrosch when he gave one of his series of musical illustrations of Wagner's operas. In his youth he was very like the Siegfried, whose sword song I have heard him play and even sing, with all the enthusiasm of the ardent music-lover which he is. In these later years the Siegfried head has whitened, but the consistently constructive life of a great conductor of a great orchestra, the benevolence and generosity of his heart, have molded his face to a serene nobility. And his wife, Margaret, has poured all her mother's ardor into her love for her own husband and children in an admirable and successful life. A late guest at their house, I have heard conversation of daughters and sons-in-law which happily reminded me of the brilliant table of their parents.

Mrs. Cameron, niece of William and John Sherman, and the young wife of the Senator from Pennsylvania, was also one of the Washington hostesses during Arthur's administration. My most vivid memory of her places her in the ballroom of the old Decatur house, then the home of General Beale, on Lafayette Square. From a dress of black velvet, adorned with a cluster of yellow jonquils, her exquisite Clytie head and shoulders emerged. With perfection of grace and manner she seemed to me a picture of accomplished seductiveness, of which her able and ambitious mind was in no way unconscious. Thus, at the very top point of my youth, with every faculty at its freshest, I met the ambassadors, judges and Cabinet Ministers who frequented these houses. It was a valuable exercise in social experience. It gave me the taste for the pleasure and profit of knowing distinguished personalities; it taught me the value of accomplishment and forever dissipated the fallacy that social power and superiority lie in small associations of unimportant contemporaries.

My father's old friend, Mr. Hitt, then and for many years the Congressman from his old home in Mt. Morris, lived in a house on a corner, where he and his wife entertained all that was best in Washington. I do not believe that I quite realized how favored I was to dine so often with the many guests at Mr. Hitt's. I was too young fully to appreciate my good fortune, although by no means too young to enjoy it or to remember each occasion. Perhaps it was a pleasure for Mr. Hitt to invite the daughter of his old friend; perhaps the contrast of Mt. Morris recollections and Washington in its dinner party mood was both piquant and agreeable.

Some of the Washington customs seem a little antiquated and peculiar as I recall them, as, for instance, the fashion of receiving in evening dress and by lamplight in the afternoons. Wednesday was the "day" of the Cabinet ladies, and Thursday of the Senators' wives, and there were also "days" of the several embassies and legations. On all these occasions the door stood widely open, with a red carpet down to the curb, and great, indeed, was the throng of "callers." Calling, in fact, in Washington has always been a duty followed with almost religious seriousness. Like the prayer wheel of Tibet, it revolves, and its feminine devotees become almost fanatical in their never relaxed observation of its routine. Newly arrived Congressmen's wives avail themselves of the opportunity of mingling with the "callers" upon their superiors of the Cabinet and the Senate, and except in rare instances do not further extend their acquaintance in Washington.

The opportunity of acquaintance with the varied types of people who represent, not only politically, but socially, all sections of our country and all countries in Europe, was often full of amusement as well as of interest. The costume worn usually by the wives of Congressmen was of black velvet, with a white bonnet tied under the chin. Thus dressed they would "entertain" one another at their various hotels or boarding-houses.

To one of these congressional boarding-houses a weary wife of a Senator once proceeded, at the end of a long day passed in the effort to return the "calls" of all the Congressmen's wives who had attended her receptions. After a long wait at the door of the house, which was on Capitol Hill, a black servant answered the bell, but he disappeared for another long period, returning at last with the desired information, written on a bit of paper, regarding the ladies whom my friend had been seeking. "Mrs. Smith is out, Mrs. Jones is taking a bath and Mrs. Robinson is dead."

An experience of my own, which included an encounter with certain Cabinet and diplomatic representatives, has always greatly diverted me. This was not in the early days of my début in Washington, but after my marriage. My husband, returning from the club, announced that he had met a certain newspaper correspondent who said that he was a friend of my father's.

56

"He is a friend, a very old friend," I replied, "and an excellent writer."

"He says he wants us to dine with him," my husband continued.

"We must surely go if he does," was my decision.

Within a few days the invitation arrived and we duly presented ourselves at a house filled with trophies from the many countries Mr. Curtis (for that was his name) had visited and written of in his newspaper columns. At table my husband found himself between Mrs. Wu, wife of the Chinese minister, and Miss Wilson, daughter of the Secretary of Agriculture. My husband's efforts at conversation elicited only grunts from the Orientally clad wife of Wu, who could speak no language but her own. With Miss Wilson, however, the topic of music was freely discussed, as she was a prospective concert singer. In the course of the conversation about music and musicians she observed: "I don't think much of that 'Robin Hood!' Do you?"

"I think I agree with you," answered my husband, "but I think, also, that I had better tell you I wrote it. You might be sorry if you said anything more."

Needless to say the conversation on Miss Wilson's side of my husband became as inaudible as that of Mrs. Wu. After dinner as I, all unaware of my husband's experiences, sat with the ladies by the drawing-room fire, while the men took their coffee in the dining room, the talk again turned upon music. Then spoke a certain Mrs. Moore of Baltimore: "Oh, Mrs. de Koven, I do admire your husband's music so much! I do think that 'Cavalleria' is the sweetest thing!" Not until my husband and I had exchanged accounts of this fruitful occasion did I understand why Miss Wilson's eyes, fixed, at first, in a stony stare, became crossed as she listened to Mrs. Moore's encomiums. But this was not the only delight of Mrs. Curtis's house. A few weeks later, seated at a "punch table" where I had been asked to officiate, Mrs. Moore approached me, her tall self, like a full-rigged ship, followed by her mother, short as her daughter was tall, but equally enthusiastic. "Oh, Mrs. de Koven, how pleased I am to meet you!" said Mrs. Moore's mother. "My daughter has talked so much about you; she says you are so elegant and dignified! and as for your husband, the great de Koven, how I wish I had met him! I would have told him how much we all owe to him. You may believe me," she continued, with crossed hands over her ample bosom, "for my heart's in my language."

It must have been about this time when, as the lessee of a house on 16th Street, two ladies called upon me. One was the wife of a naval officer who lived in the neighborhood and the other was Mrs. Benton of Missouri. On entering the room the first lady exclaimed: "I thought I would call upon you, Mrs. de Koven, for I know that you are a stranger. I hope you like my neighborly ways. Your landlady is such a sweet woman and a great friend of mine." After some reluctant admission on my part, in answer to her friendly inquiries, that I had been in Washington before, she relapsed into a somewhat disconcerted silence and I turned to her companion.

"Have you been in Washington long, Mrs. Benton?" I asked.

"Oh no," she replied. "I am from the West."

"Don't let that trouble you," was my answer, "for I am also. I was born in Chicago."

Thus reassured, Mrs. Benton continued: "My husband is a grandson of Thomas H. Benton. They wanted to make him Governor, but I told him I preferred Washington to Jefferson City; but I might as well have stayed in Missouri for all anybody knows I am here."

During this conversation an observing New York friend, Mr. Elliot Gregory, had been announced, and I shall never forget his expression as he listened from behind the sofa, or his later comments upon Mrs. Benton's casual dealings with governorships and seats in our legislative body. A few weeks after the visit of these ladies, I met the wife of the naval officer at the house of a Mrs. Rochester, sister of New York's Bradley Martin. Mrs. Rochester was herself the wife of an army officer and her "day" was attended by ladies of the army and navy services. As I sat in my chair I perceived the determined figure and the black-eyed physiognomy of my navy "caller" and addressed her as she passed me.

"Who is this speaking?" was her question as she looked condescendingly down upon me.

"I am Mrs. de Koven," I answered, "and you were kind enough to call upon me a few weeks ago."

"But Mrs. de Koven is a blonde," she quite incredulously replied. Again, as I laughingly protested that

I had not dyed my hair since she had visited me, she continued, "But you look so young with your hat on." This conversation had at last attracted the attention of Mrs. Rochester and she confirmed my identity to the lady, who followed my exit with an amusing expression of discomfiture.

The first time I saw Mr. Dawes I sat next him at dinner and greatly enjoyed a conversation of rapid-fire commentary with that very original banker, composer, and story-writer, then in the early and freshest years of his successful career. A visitor from Hawaii was also of this party, his dark eyes suffused with his Pacific-island blood as if dipped in ink. "They call America God's country," he declared, "but I tell you mine is angels' country and when I get though with my business here you won't see me for the dust." So much for the superiority of the angels over the Deity and his preference for Honolulu.

At this time in Washington the diplomatic representatives were very attractive and the city was so small that one met them daily. The Marchese Imperiale, so long Italian ambassador to London, was secretary of his Washington embassy and an accomplished type of Italian good looks, very popular and agreeable. Sir Lionel Sackville-West was the English ambassador, and at the big and gloomy British Embassy I first saw his daughter Victoria. It was the regular "day" at the Embassy but no one was present to help her "receive." That much apprehension regarding her acceptance by Washington had troubled this brown-clad convent girl was evident as she falteringly emerged from behind one

PICNIC TO MOUNT VERNON

Left to right, top row: General Macomb, ..., Miss Kilburn, Mrs. Clover, Alan Arthur, Miss Maud Crowly; ......

Second row: Miss Grace Farwell, Miss M. Kilburn, Mrs. MacPherson, Miss Anna Farwell, Lieut. Fred Paine; *Bottom row:* Mr. Arthur Farwell, ..., Lieutenant Babcock, Lieutenant Rae, Lieutenant Clover, Mr. Walter Farwell

of the great doors of the drawing room to greet me. At this time she was as slim as a lily and as white, shy and almost inarticulate. When Lady Orford, later met in Florence on my wedding journey, asked me if "those children of Sir Lionel had been accepted in Washington," I recalled and related this first meeting with the eldest daughter who had been summoned to become the chatelaine of her father's post. "They are not legitimate," Lady Orford continued. "I was in Madrid when Sackville-West was a secretary and I often saw Pepita dance, who was their mother." It was a very short time before Victoria, whose fears of her acceptance by a very kindly Washington had soon been allayed, took complete possession of the Embassy and apparently of her father. Invitations to balls came in her own handwriting, and all the unofficial correspondence of the Embassy was under her supervision. It was, indeed, a fact whispered in Washington that for once she had omitted to look over her father's letters, and this once included the indiscreet letter of criticism of the President which cost him his recall and retirement from the diplomatic service. The remarkable taste, as a collector and inventor of various saleable novelties of house decoration, which Lady Sackville later developed was accompanied by so great a pleasure in devising and selling them, that she told me, when I saw her years later in London, that she was only happy in her shop and was greatly bored by the Knole house parties. The prose and poetry of her daughter, representing an even greater development of artistic instinct, has descended,

61

doubtless, from her grandmother, the beautiful Spanish dancer.

Mrs. MacPherson, wife of the Senator from New Jersey, I recall with many admiring and tender thoughts. Had she been a school-teacher before her rather dour but devoted Scotch husband had brought her triumphantly to Washington? So it was related. But no one I have ever known was so passionate a lover of life, so intelligently worldly, or so kind, although that kindness had a touch of sadness which I could not fathom. She was more than beautiful, for her face, intensely alive, her lovely head with its smooth dark hair, her contralto voice, now mocking, now full of melancholy music, expressed a rare personality. As I now realize, she sought me for my youth and my innocence of all the experiences which had, too soon, exhausted her own vitality. At one dinner at her house I saw Bourke Cochran at the end of the long table and many times in the years of our later acquaintance we recalled our mutual impressions of each other. The massive gray head of the Irish lawyer and politician came to be very familiar to the American public, which knew him as one of the few men who deserved the name of orator. As I saw him in that winter of 1881 his hair was as black and lustrous as that of any Irish colleen and his eyes as blue, while the deep rose of his cheeks spoke of abounding health and vigor. A very different Bourke from the dear friend of my later life, and one whom, I imagine, no one but myself can now remember. It is a pleasure to recall his affection for my parents and my lovely sister, his own pleasure in his Long Island house, his always eloquent and witty talk on country sojourns at my father's house and his own. "Beloved Anna," I can hear him say in that rich voice of his, as he would greet me after some long absence or separation, expressing the loyalty and the long recollections of so many years. He was one of Mrs. MacPherson's devoted friends and never forgot her, although she died soon after our early acquaintance with her in Washington, leaving no one who quite resembled her. And what a delight in the humor of Washington and its familiar and easy customs she showed! "If you want any work done here, my dear," she used to say, "don't forget that you must treat all these black people as friends. Look at this letter from the little man who repairs my furniture; he signs himself, 'Your loving carpenter.'" Among the collection of letters, invitations, and signed menu cards is this typewritten invitation of one of Senator MacPherson's constituents and the lament at his refusal:

HOTEL NORMANDIE. WASHINGTON, D. C.
May 5th 1892.

Mr. & Mrs. George F. Stackhouse of Palmyra—New Jersey, cordially solicit your company to lunch, at high noon, Saturday 7th instant at this hotel.

Your company is further requested to make up a driving party (of an even *two dozen*) to attend the Spring Meeting of the Washington Driving Club.

à la California.

R. S. V. P.

HOTEL NORMANDIE. WASHINGTON, D. C.

Mr. & Mrs. Geo. F. Stackhouse beg to express their unadulterated regrets at the absence of Mr. & Mrs. M'Pherson, at tomorrow's lunch and coaching party, as it was their earnest desire that Palmyra—Burlington County, N. J. (their recent home) should have been represented in the person of "our Senator" and the Hon. Mrs.

May 6th —92.

Sir Julian Pauncefote took Sir Lionel Sackville-West's place in Washington and was long at the British Embassy. Sir Julian, afterwards Lord Pauncefote, was a very kindly and very typical Englishman; tall and courtly, wise and tactful as his predecessor had been indiscreet, he was the best loved of all the long line of British ambassadors to our country. To all the Embassies, to the houses of the Cabinet ladies, to Mrs. Blaine's, Mrs. Frelinghuysen's, and Mrs. Cameron's we were carried, in those days, in the little "herdics" which were the Washington hansoms. They were very convenient vehicles, like small omnibuses, with facing seats and at the end a door for dumping passengers, and twenty-five cents was the tariff. But the drivers had a paternal care of us, and if we lingered on Sunday nights, at some festivity, past ten o'clock, would often send in a message that it was time for us to go home.

There was, as I remember this first winter in Washington, after Mrs. Logan's invitation to the church sociable had so luckily opened its doors to me, no day and no evening without its pleasures. The older women had their favorite débutantes, and one of these, a certain Mrs. "General" Ricketts, had chosen me. She was not of Cabinet rank, but a Southern woman gay and persistently hospitable. I often used to assist her in "receiving" on her regular afternoons in my long trailing dress of Chinese pink, with the "Prince of Wales feathers," helping to serve the punch and the hot Southern cakes, to an exhilarated company of army officers and tireless female "callers."

And there were picnics to Mount Vernon, and water parties on the Potomac, and endless strolls on the redbrick sidewalks and long walks in the country, with one or another friend or "admirer," until the end of the session, when Congress would adjourn and the curtain come down on the hot and empty summer in Washington.

It was all so pleasant, so really interesting, when the background was historical and many of one's companions were making history themselves.

One of the most striking of the many personages of that time was a certain General Brewster of Arthur's Cabinet. In his early childhood he had pulled his little sister from the fire, saving her life, but carrying ever after, as the price of his youthful heroism, a face hopelessly disfigured. He was brilliantly successful as a lawyer, and had attained the high position that he occupied as Attorney General, when I used often to see him in the streets and drawing rooms of Washington. He wore always deep ruffles of lace over his beautiful hands, a silent but most significant indication that this *"homme qui rit"* was a despairing lover of all things beautiful.

An incident which concerned me occurred one evening at the White House, at the close of a Diplomatic reception, when my father was talking to the President in the Blue Room, then almost empty of guests. I was standing alone when I felt the influence of some thought or

intention which seemed directed to me. I turned where
I stood, and perceived that General Brewster was coming toward me. I could not divine his purpose, as I had
never known him personally. "My dear," he exclaimed,
quite simply, as he reached my side and looked at me
from that pitiful mask of a face, "I have been watching
you all winter. I think your face has much character.
I hope you will be happy. That is all." And he left
me so quickly that I had no opportunity of uttering the
thanks and the sympathy which would have been inadequate enough to one who had learned so profoundly of
life. A blessing I thought it, and did deeply thank him
for his words to the young adventurer.

Strange, uncouth figures, hangers-on to the medley
of "representatives" from all parts of the country, were
constantly seen in the Capitol and in the corridors of the
hotels. "Jim" Fair, the Senator from Nevada, was a
strange enough occupant of high position, gained only
through the fortune which his casual pick and shovel had
dug out of a silver mountain-side; he was indeed so lost
and helpless among his fellow legislators that he abandoned the sessions of the Senate and spent his days in
the company of the small red-headed boy of a certain
Representative Crowley. With this excited attendant
he used to patrol Pennsylvania Avenue, throwing his
superfluous dollars into the ditches to be scrambled for
by young Crowley or any other urchin who might dis-
pute for his largess.

But the said youthful Crowley was not the only satel-
lite of Senator Fair. In the Arlington Hotel, where I
used to see him daily in the dining room with his blond

wife and two black-haired little girls, now Mrs. Oelrichs and Mrs. W. K. Vanderbilt, Jr., there lurked a certain very doubtful-looking reporter of a Chicago evening newspaper, by name Hanscom. This individual limped on one short leg, but he was by no means deterred by this disability from an astounding and most original series of activities. To Senator Fair he attached himself and soon assumed the rôle of "guide and philosopher." As the Arlington Hotel was his *Champs de bataille,* its importance as a social center was paramount. Thus thinking, Hanscom proposed to the Senator that he should give a dinner to the young ladies who resided in this glittering abode. No lack of acquaintance among these young ladies was to him a deterrent. My sister Grace, then just fourteen, was invited with me. One "young" lady, quite unknown to us all, and already gray haired, was also included. Another, as I recall her, but not her name, came clad in a long "trail" of black velvet, with a blue-satin bodice, as unrelated to her dress as she was to her sister guests. Through his Western associations, Senator Fair also invited the two most brilliant young women of the capital, that universal conqueror of men, Miss Emily Beale, and with her, her rival in wit and seductiveness, Miss Bayard. Miss Davis of West Virginia, sister-in-law of Senator Elkins, was also a member of this strange party.

To receive the guests in proper attire, Hanscom importuned my father for the wherewithal to purchase a dress suit, and, failing this, adorned himself as best he could, with a flowing white necktie over his reportorial clothes. Thus welcomed by the Senator and the reporter, the invited young ladies assembled in the appointed private dining room. Flowers and wines of the most extravagant variety were provided for their honor. But the duty of greeting his fair guests proved too great a task for the Senator's experience. When he had uttered, "How are you, my good girl? How is your good father?" some six or seven times, he retired in dismay, and relegated the privilege of receiving to Miss Davis of West Virginia.

I found myself at table beside Miss Beale, and then and there began a friendship of more than twenty years with that unforgettable personality, whose burning loyalty, whose whole-hearted devotion to her friends, was by no means unaccompanied by biting commentaries on the Washington spectacle she so long dominated and amused.

I can see that dinner table now, with the Senator at one end and the reporter at the other, and my little sister's bewildered brown eyes as she silently regarded the table, illuminated by the vivid elegance of Miss Beale and Miss Bayard—Miss Davis's dark eyes and dark hair, the velvet-clad unknown, and the gray-haired old maid, also unknown. Pretty and blond Maude Crowley, then engaged to President Arthur's son, was also there, blooming for a brief moment in flower-like loveliness, before the galloping consumption, which so soon ended her life.

A dinner party such as this would never have been assembled, it is quite safe to say, in any clime, under any skies other than those of Washington. Another dinner, quite as extraordinary, was given in Washington a few years later. To this I was unluckily unbidden, but was duly informed that the once powerful Senator Cushman Davis of Minnesota sat beside his wife at the head of the table, while at the other end, placed together, were two bewildered ambassadors, with Senators and Representatives making up the sides, and all served by small boys who "paged," as in the halls of Congress, bringing wines and viands at the request of the guests. What indeed must have been the reflections of the ambassadors regarding a society which could alternate such a complete ignorance of custom with the perfection of the many other dinner tables which they nightly attended?

In this connection, the familiar compliment from Europeans as to the adaptability of American women, may call out the expression of my own opinion, founded on many years of observation of this adaptability in the wives of Representatives and Cabinet Ministers, even the Presidents' wives. Unless these women have been early accustomed to the habits and usages of so-called society in their own home, I do not think that they have been able to adapt themselves to those usages when they have been called upon to do so. Too generally, the stern and narrow conditions of the lives of these women, before their husbands have obtained the prizes of toil and effort, have crystallized manner and speech and dried up the youthful plasticity which might have been otherwise capable of adaption to the new conditions.

One Senator's wife, for instance, who later rose to greater heights, with ill-concealed disgust pointed out to me a photograph of her daughter standing quietly among a bevy of curled and befeathered beauties of her home town, with the remark, "Mame she don't know how to poise."

The men, on the other hand, although retaining the "Western" accent too generally spread over the larger part of America by our Yorkshire ancestors, who had exactly this accent, do acquire a courtesy and ease of manner born of long association with politics and politicians. "Uncle" Joe Cannon, long Speaker of the House of Representatives, was as astutely skillful and polished as a diplomat, with the voice of his own Western prairies.

CHAPTER FIVE

WASHINGTON (CONTINUED)

IT has long been admitted that the short administration of General Arthur was more agreeable than any which preceded it, and I do not think I am wrong in venturing the opinion, based on an experience of several which have followed, that its quite unique delightfulness has never since been equaled. History establishes the first proposition, and contemporary testimony the second. Dolly Madison, the hostess of the White House during the war of 1812, has left to history a delightful figure of wit which was her own happy endowment, and of amiability, which has the characteristic of the South, her birthplace. But although she gayly led the "routs" of the little Washington of those days, in her bright brocades and her turban with its diamond aigrette, although her humor never failed her even when the English came and burned the capital, she was forced to bear with the crudest and most uncomfortable war-time conditions and the days of her supremacy were few and stormy.

After the death of Madison she lived until a great age in what was long known as the Coutts Mansion, in Washington and there Adelaide Coutts, who was her greatniece, passed her childhood. This lovely child, who became later the wife of Stephen A. Douglas, was far more beautiful than her famous aunt, and her portrait, with its magnificent brown eyes and its radiant smile, may be seen in the beauty albums of the year 1860. As the young widow of Senator Douglas she married Robert Williams, and their youngest daughter, Mildred, is my sister-in-law, Mrs. Walter Farwell. How short is our history, I have often reflected, when I have heard her quote her mother's anecdotes of "Aunt Dolly" and even much of what "Aunt Dolly" used to say. In a series of contemporary letters published about sixty years after her death, an engaging impression of "Aunt Dolly" at Montpelier is depicted.

A young girl, fatigued by a long ride and a stranger to Mrs. Madison, stopped at her door. After the custom of the always hospitable Virginians, she was most kindly made welcome, taken to the hostess's own bedroom, and invited to rest on her bed in her riding habit, where Mrs. Madison brought her many sweet cakes and a warm drink, plying her the while with gay talk, so that her visitor was not only refreshed, but recorded her thrilling experience to her relative, who included it in his narrative of the war period of 1812.

Southern manners, rising from the luxury and intimacy of life in those lovely houses of Virginia, linked as they were by the abounding hospitality which prevailed up to the Civil War, were indeed far more gracious than those of Puritan New England. Those manners were again shown in the White House during the Presidency of Buchanan, who was assisted by his niece, Miss Harriet Lane Johnson, in all the White House hospitalities. I saw this lady in Washington in her old age in the winter of 1882-83. White-haired and beautifully dressed, with jewels and old lace, she preserved the dignity and charm of her well-remembered reign.

During Buchanan's time Washington had become a larger and more developed capital than in the preceding years of Jackson and Pierce, and was filled with the Southern people who had made it their home. But the streets were still unpaved and the city hardly more than an overgrown village, straggling among its little parks between the Capitol on its hill, and the White House. No marked social gifts had been manifested by the immediate predecessors of President Arthur. Thus when this little-known individual, who had been placed on Garfield's ticket to placate the great State of New York, was raised to the Presidency by Garfield's assassination, Washington was presented with the greatest gentleman, with the exception of Washington himself and possibly Buchanan, who had ever occupied the Executive Mansion. With a great height of most graceful manhood, Chester Arthur was truly courtly and an accomplished host. He delighted to assemble the agreeable people of the capital and of the country at the White House and received them with inimitable charm and amiability. Still small in size and conducted with great ease and familiarity, Washington society was at its very best.

In the morning the flowering parks were filled with groups of friends, meeting as in the country for walks or conversation. In the evening they again met, not to dance or to play cards, not to sit down to elaborate suppers, but to talk, and when this talk was contributed by the individuals who composed this society, it was delightful to listen, and a privilege and honor to share in it.

The Senate, while by no means the brilliant oratorical body of the days of Webster, Clay, and Calhoun, was dominated already by that group of the all-powerful Republican party which was later to gain the title of the "Old Guard." They were far less dramatic in their eloquence; they were perhaps far less unselfish in their type of patriotism than their famous predecessors, but they ably conducted the administration of a great and victorious party, firmly in the saddle after the war, and they were the representatives of the great business interests which were expanding with unexampled prosperity with the rapid growth of the country. They were indeed both able and constructive, and as in the case of Aldrich, closed the era of their long control with measures such as that for the reform of the banking system, which proved that practical statesmanship may have its place even beside the thunderous eloquence of a Webster.

Nelson Aldrich, from Rhode Island, was already in Washington, in the winter of 1881-82, and I often saw him at the Arlington Hotel, where he also was stopping. Sometimes during the weeks of December, before his family had joined him at the capital, it was his pleasure to invite me, with an older friend, to little theater parties, after which we would partake of the "oyster stews" for which the Southern cooking was famous. We supped together in that white dining room of the Arlington Hotel, white as to walls and columns and china and napery, picked out, as I so well remember, by

74

the ebony-hued waiters in their black garments and by
Aldrich's own striking dark head. I cannot imagine
that my schoolgirl's conversation could have greatly
interested him, but he was then and always interested
in human nature and an indulgent and faithful friend,
as he many times proved during the twenty-five years
of our acquaintance. His manner with women was a
mixture of shyness and audacity. He would catch his
underlip in his white teeth and laugh like a boy
over some feminine retort or sally, enjoying with perfect good humor his own occasional discomfiture. Not
only in the earliest period of our acquaintance, but many
times in later years, I have found that he was willing to
relegate politics to a temporary eclipse for the opportunity of testing the quality of the feminine mind. On
one well-remembered five-hour journey from Washington to New York our unending conversation was
watched with increasing irritation by a political associate, who had evidently intended to discuss some matter of party politics with his superior. But this was in
the year 1900, and nearly twenty years had gone by
since we partook of oyster suppers at the Arlington. In
this first season of 1881 he was in his early forties and
seemed taller, with his still youthful figure, than in the
succeeding years. In appearance he was unusually
striking. Dark eyes of extraordinary keenness, brows
and hair as black as an Italian's, quite clearly expressed
the personality of the man who for many years was the
undisputed ruler of the Senate. His knowledge of men
was quick and accurate and his command of his party
adherents and agents singularly authoritative, as I have

often observed, when like a general he issued his orders to the waiting subordinates in his crowded committee room. But his knowledge and control of men were transcended by his financial ability, finally expressed in the famous banking bill which it was Wilson's undeserved opportunity to make into law during the Democratic administration.

In this connection I may be permitted to state that a financial ability, marked enough to merit General Grant's choice of my father as Secretary of the Treasury, was expressed in a bill for banking reform, printed in the Congressional records of the year 1882, which is essentially the same as Aldrich's bill. General Logan's senatorial opposition to my father's appointment as Secretary of the Treasury was one of his many acts of hostility to the man who succeeded him, but Aldrich's admission to me of his pleasure in discussing financial measures with my father, and the latter's membership of the Finance Committee of the Senate, are confirmatory testimony regarding this tardy but truthful statement. My father's sensitiveness, like the bloom on a fruit, was never brushed off in all his long political life, and with it was a modesty, an inherent inability to urge any personal advantage, which seriously handicapped his political preferment. The advice, in the words of one of his political cronies, "He that bloweth not his own trumpet, the same shall not be blowed," was never followed by himself.

In 1881 Eugene Hale was here also in his young prime, wittier far than Aldrich and master of sarcastic and cruel eloquence, a formidable antagonist in debate

and a very catholic lover of women. His wife regarded
her husband with cool eyes of amusement and understanding, as I could not but realize, as she related to me
a conversation with the delightfully impertinent William Walter Phelps, who was at that time in Washington, after his absence in Vienna as our ambassador. Mr.
Phelps had a most amusing physiognomy, his hair cut
like a schoolgirl's bang, hung low over a pair of witty
brown eyes with which he would examine every detail
of feminine dress, as in his drawling voice he would pro-
pound audacious questions and personal remarks.
"Why," he asked Mrs. Hale, "are your eyes so happy
when you know that Eugene is running after other
women?" Many times in my girlhood I dined at her
house and many times, twenty years later, I used to visit
her to recall the earlier days, and found her always
serene, calmly sufficient in herself, even after the passing
of the power of her husband and his contemporaries.

Hoar of Massachusetts was also in the Senate with
his patriarchal Puritan appearance, ready to oppose,
even to his own physical exhaustion, any measure which
did not correspond with his strict standards of ethics.
Senator Lodge, his colleague of Massachusetts, was slim
and elegant in profile, highly intellectual and in the heyday of a long political career. He was better equipped
mentally than he was in character for the party
politics in which he was too often swayed by personal
ambitions and prejudices. McMillan of Ohio, always
my father's reliable coadjutor, was the type of a successful Western business man, endowed with an eminent
share of common sense and an able and loyal Repub-

lican. Allison of Missouri was thirty years in the Senate, growing old in the "Republican Guard" and with his white-haired dignity, his singularly urbane demeanor, decorated an assembly of individuals of equal mental and physical distinction.

The appearance of our Upper Chamber at this time was indeed an honor to the country. At present, the Senate Chamber, filled as it is with lounging men, ill clad and, in their irregular and undeveloped types, representing their not too long past arrival by way of the steerage, is more like a railroad waiting room than a debating house of legislature. So have our fathers sold their birthright for the cheap labor whose delegates now sit in the seats of the mighty at Washington. The descendants and legitimate successors of the men who founded our Republic were long worthy to sustain that noble work of constructive government, but when the election of Senators was thrown, not into the hands of the people, but into those of secret political "rings," dignity began to disappear from the Senate and the delegates of the enlarging foreign population of low birth and origin and lower ideals have brought the once pride of our country, the envied place of all honorable servants of its welfare, to this low position and to the defiant obstruction of wise executive measures which we have too often seen in later years.

In 1881 Cullom of Illinois was also there, later my father's colleague and in the middle years of his long service as Senator. He had a very characteristic New England type of personality, although mid-Western in residence and origin. Strictly honorable in all his actions, political and personal, a loyal Republican and conservative in his opinions, he was capable of the warmest devotion to his friends, as was shown by the letter he wrote to me after my father's death, when he told his daughter that her father had been for thirty years like his own brother, and that for generosity and loyalty he was the noblest man he had ever known.

It may be pardoned that adoring daughter if she relates that while in the Lower House of Congress her father, whose keen eyes of quick perception and kindness, whose deep, musical voice and contagious humor, made him instantly exceedingly popular with all his colleagues, was called "the handsomest man in the House of Representatives."

My association with these political personages was based on their warm friendship for my father and made possible by the delightful informality of the mode of entertainment then prevalent in Washington during those two winters of 1882-83. I was doubtless quite seriously handicapped, however, by the reputation of too much blue in my stocking. My mother had decided that French was not a useful language and had sent me into what she might have imagined would be a *milieu* where it would be essential, without one word of the diplomatic tongue at my disposal. But the Greek Testament which she had always longed to be able to read in the original was firmly clasped in my hand.

"Do you speak Greek?" was the eager question of two young men on first meeting me. "We have had a bet all winter that you could." But youth is always youth and mine was intensely responsive to the new and strangely contrasting experiences into which I was thrown, without any preparation, from the Puritan stronghold of my school days. I was grave enough sometimes, and inclined to take everything *au grand sérieux,* but very confiding and simple, and capable of keen enjoyment. Perfect health and the support of my father's pride and affection added to my happiness. Well dressed I was also, according to the curious fashion of the time which decreed long trains for afternoon gowns and "dinner dresses" for girls in their "teens," fortunately not worn at dances, where we just swept the floor with our tulle skirts; and low-cut bodices showed shoulders rounded with youth.

Memories are very persistent, as I found in the winter of 1924, when one dancing partner, long a white-haired general, said, "I remember how Sandy Rodgers said to me, 'Miss Farwell has a new hat. Let's cross the street and see how she looks in it,'" and then, with all his old loyalty looking out from the clearest and bravest eyes in the world, and with his old humorous twist of the lips, he declared, "We were very glad to have you with us, you know."

Only a month, and this gallant old friend was no longer with us, and I cherish this little final conversation with General Macomb with the affectionate appreciation which he called forth from all who knew him. His cousin, Mrs. Forbes, whom I knew very intimately in 1880-81 as "Lulie" Meigs, and whose house, built like an Italian villa, I so often visited, had an exceedingly marked individuality. She lived at this time alone with her father, Quartermaster General of the Northern

MRS. HENRY DE KOVEN
FLORENCE, 1884

DR. HENRY DE KOVEN
FLORENCE, 1884

Army during the Civil War, and architect of the wings of the Capitol and of the Patent Office. His house, which, strangely, I afterward leased and remodeled, had a drawing room and dining room supported by Ionic columns reminiscent of the Capitol. Admirals and generals were my friend's ancestors and no one more perfectly personified their honor, their loyalty, and their high flashing temper. Humor also she possessed in good measure, and as fully appreciated it, as she expressed in a long letter written during our renewed acquaintance in Switzerland after the war of 1914— thirty-four years later. She congratulated me on having developed this valuable quality, which she avowed had been invisible in my youth.

She was married for only a short time to the celebrated war correspondent, Archibald Forbes, of 1870 fame, and had the sad privilege of nursing his broken health and old age, passing a lonely widowhood in England and Europe. During the war she occupied her wonderfully skilled hands in making exquisite needlework to help all war sufferers, working far into her many wakeful nights. I left her at the end of another period of intimate association in Vevey, in the year 1920, and heard from the lips of her cousin, General Macomb, during that last affectionate talk with him, of her death in 1923. They were both representatives of the very best America can produce, of old and gallant lineage and all its interests and standards, and it is my pride that I knew and loved them and that they loved me, with a loyalty utterly and constantly faithful, according to their noble natures.

A MUSICIAN AND HIS WIFE

I may be pardoned for dwelling on the characters of these dearly loved friends, for they were of that order of Americans of excellent origin and traditions who before and during our Civil War believed that their inherited qualities were fitly used in the service of their country. Their example has not been followed in these later years when the peaceful country and the unattractive conditions of army posts have, not unnaturally, deterred ambitious American youth from following the profession of a soldier. The navy service, while offering more opportunities, is also ill paid by the government, so that it has scarcely more recruits from the descendants of the original Colonists who, by right of good birth and its instincts and practice, should be recognized as typically American.

The mothers of General Macomb and Mrs. Forbes were both daughters of Admiral Rodgers, and through him connected by descent with Commodore Perry of glorious memory, and with Mrs. August Belmont, his great-granddaughter. (Mrs. August Belmont was the daughter of Commodore Perry, and niece of others of glorious memory).

CHAPTER SIX

IN March, 1883, I returned to Chicago, or rather Lake Forest, finding the quiet of the little Western suburb very depressing after so much of interest and amusement in the capital. A few weeks at Bar Harbor during the summer months diverted me, although the restricted food in the barrack of a hotel which was the best that luxurious colony then offered was little adapted to nourish my active young appetite. But there were water excursions by moonlight, and there was a quota of Washington friends such as Mr. Blaine and his family, and endless walks and drives along the pine-grown roads near the sea, and, as must happen at such an age, there were questions of marriage, disturbing and exciting. Then I returned to Lake Forest and soon to the house on Prairie Avenue which my father had rented for the winter of 1883-84.

There were "classes" in a barn-like hall for dancing instruction, organized and attended by no less a remarkable company than that of the men who had built up the city's prosperity and who had had no time for dancing in their youth. Robert Lincoln, Franklin Mac Veagh, Mr. Pullman, Mr. Fairbanks, General Sheridan, Marshall Field—all names to conjure with in the history of Chicago and the country—then and there took their first lessons in dancing. "Oh, General,"

83

said one very flattering lady, "your dancing is the poetry of motion." "D —— it, madam," replied the hero of Sheridan's ride, who was vainly struggling with a polka, "don't make fun of me!" I was so slim and light in those days that I was sometimes swung quite off my feet by one or another of those able and enthusiastic dancers. But it was all fun and gayety, even if our supper consisted only of lemonade and doughnuts.

Then there were the evening receptions, when—shall I confess it—Chicago's first ladies appeared in high satin dresses and bonnets tied under their chins. At one of these receptions I wore the only low-cut dress in the company, and in this first caught the eye of my future husband approaching me with his cousin, Miss Louise de Koven, on his arm. With this first meeting or sight of each other, for we did not speak that evening, my new life began. Among the pleasant occupations of this winter one incident holds its recollections very clearly. I had just announced my engagement when I was invited, with my *fiancé,* to come to Mrs. Franklin Mac Veagh's to meet Matthew Arnold. He sat after dinner in a deep chair by the fire with a Persian cat on his knee. Brought up by my hostess to talk with her guest, I spoke of his poem, "Self-Dependence."

"I composed this," he told me, "on a moonlit night when I was crossing the Channel. I was much troubled about religion," he added, musingly. Then awakening from his after-dinner reverie, he began a series of questions about myself.

"What are you thinking of doing?" he asked.

"I am going to be married quite soon," I told him,

"and going to Italy—to Florence—on my wedding journey."

"Oh! you are going to be married? And who is the fortunate—?" His words were accompanied by an expression of genuine interest, but cut short by the first chords struck on the piano by my husband-to-be.

"He plays very well, that young man. Who is he?" again queried Mr. Arnold.

"The young man I am going to marry," I answered. Then, dispossessing the cat of her place on his knee, Mr. Arnold turned a really scrutinizing gaze first on the player and then on me.

"I should like to know what becomes of those two young people," he said afterwards to Mrs. Mac Veagh. "They are both very promising and interesting."

In the spring of 1884, May the 1st, I was married in my father's house, Lake Forest, to Reginald de Koven. A word here about the family of this musician and composer may not be inappropriate.

Von Koven, or de Koven, is the Hanoverian name of a family whose representatives were soldiers as far back as the Crusades. In the records of the family occur many names of abbesses and priests, for the de Kovens were often as religious as they were soldierly. The martial strain expressed itself in Captain John Louis de Koven, who had already been enrolled in the British army before the war of the American Revolution. His father was the military governor of the district which contained the little town of Eisnach, his birthplace, and the home of various others of his family. Captain John Louis de Koven was placed in command of a Hessian regiment hired to fight in the Revolution and thus he came to the Colonies.

But Captain de Koven was soon captured with his regiment on board the ship *Badger* in the bay of New York. He was given his liberty on parole, and proceeded to the elm-shaded town of Middletown, Connecticut, and there married a Miss Sebor. After a short period, and at the close of the war, he was forced to return to Hanover to look after his property. The seas had been swept remarkably clear of English vessels during the war, when our privateers were far more active than the ships of the navy, and communication was rare and uncertain. Several years elapsed before the Hanoverian officer could find a return passage to America. When he did return he found himself the unhappy hero of what was a veritable Enoch Arden story. His wife, persuaded that he would never return and thinking his absence only attributable to his death, had been married again to an old and persistent suitor. When, as the family tradition relates, the lover and husband returned, she was utterly crushed "and never after lifted her head." She was very beautiful, so it is said, and proud of her birth and breeding. Captain de Koven wrote a letter to the bishop who had married him, recalling the fact and explaining that he considered it his duty to leave his wife in her new relation, and went to live in Canada, where, according to other letters, he lived in lonely sadness, dying at last of the mysterious malady called *tic douleureux*.

No portraits exist of Captain John or of his son Captain Henry Louis de Koven, but it is related that they were tall men, fair in complexion and hair, and both very handsome. Captain Henry married his cousin, Miss Sebor, whose mother was Margaret Winthrop, daughter of John Still Winthrop the Colonial governor. Henry Louis de Koven built the house which still stands by the river in Middletown and there established a prosperous shipping business. He sailed, as did other merchants, to the Indies, and in the War of 1812 was in command of privateers. His fortune with excellent but too early prevision was largely invested in land in Chicago, and he became "land poor" in consequence. The street called after his name was afterward celebrated as containing the stable where the cow kicked over the lantern which started the Chicago fire. His children were ten, the eldest my husband's father, who due to the restricted circumstances of the family, himself conducted the education of his younger brothers and sisters. James de Koven was an example of the excellence of this instruction and became a very well known clergyman and educator. The devotion to religion which characterized the grandchildren of Margaret Winthrop may have been inherited through her from that fiercest of royal governors, the redoubtable John Winthrop. The theocracy which he established in Massachusetts was a strictly ordered rule, based on his belief that one chosen of God and possessed of aristocratic pretensions was doubly privileged to exclude all outsiders either of belief or of birth.

Henry and James de Koven, Mary, the eldest daughter, and Frances, the youngest, were deeply, even enthusiastically, religious, but a simplicity of nature and

87

a redeeming humor preserved them all from any extravagance of intolerance or pretension. The humor and enthusiasm of the family became, in James de Koven, brilliant wit and inspiring eloquence. He was very "high church" in his doctrines, and founded, in Racine, Wisconsin, a little college where this form of doctrine and service were promulgated. These doctrines were not approved of by the Episcopal Church in America at this time, and his advocacy of them cost him his dignity as a bishop. He was always, however, called Bishop de Koven. As to his personal influence on all the students of Racine, it was so potent and so lovable that all who experienced it blessed his memory. He was, in truth, one of the best known and best loved teachers of his day. He died while still in early manhood, and deprived of his inspiring influence, the little church school soon sank into insignificance.

Another son, William, was a commander in the navy and, according to an old admiral whom I met in Washington, was very attractive and most excellent company. He also died early. Another son, John, whom I knew long and well, was a banker in Chicago. His only child, Louise, now Mrs. Bowen, has long been an honor to her family. She has founded schools and institutions in connection with the Children's Court in Chicago, served as a member of the last Republican campaign committee, and has lately refused the nomination as mayor of Chicago.

All the de Koven family possessed qualities of marked individuality. The five aunts of my husband had delightful old-fashioned manners and a naïve and delicious humor. They adored one another's society, and when, as a new member of the family, I made relationships outside the charmed circle it was considered a curious and unnecessary proceeding. Mrs. Dyer, the eldest aunt, lived for some years in Chicago. There my mother met her, and so greatly admired her eloquence in prayer at the various meetings where they became acquainted, that when I announced my engagement to her nephew she was greatly pleased.

"If he is anything like his aunt," my mother said, "you could not do better."

Mrs. Wadsworth was far less religious, but had the entrancing naïveté of the family. She married a man of large fortune and was very generous to those who pleased her. Her remarks about herself were very characteristic of the family, who all commented upon their own gifts and graces with no departure from strict verity, but with disconcerting frankness.

"No," she said to me one day, "I do not like that portrait; it has not my sweet smile."

"Of course they all loved me when I was a child, I was such a little darling," said another of these delightful aunts, Mrs. Dickey. "Aunt Fanny," as we all called Mrs. Dickey, was, if I may confess it, my favorite. Her husband, Judge Dickey, had both position and worldly fortune, and in representing the first and dispensing the latter his wife was, in every sense, beyond praise. She was as great a lady as I ever knew, very happy in her religious faith, and exquisitely kind and charitable. An amusing expression of her equal appreciation of religion and of worldly pleasure was the organization of a Bible class for her young Newport friends, which was invariably followed by dancing. Her house on Fifth Avenue, as well as that in Newport, was directed with most careful attention. Her table was bountiful and beautifully set with old family silver, and when only attended by my husband she took his arm to go in to dinner. She was one of that disappearing order of American gentlewomen whose memory is green. I went to her house in New York soon after I was engaged and was conducted to her boudoir, where I found her dressed in all the glory of purple velvet and pearls. Her gray hair was piled on her lovely head, and her blue eyes regarded me with a gaze which was benevolent and scrutinizing. "Please sit here, my dear," she said. "I desire to watch the expression of your face while you talk." But how inexpressibly kind was this rather frightening lady! I often stayed, in the early years of my marriage, at her house in Newport, and often I drove along Ocean Avenue behind her fat and faithful old coachman in her victoria, as she greeted her friends, also driving, quite beautifully dressed, for what was in those days a very important part of Newport life. On my last visit she gave me a touching proof of her kindness. It was a little gift such as she was constantly minded to make me of a number of gold pieces. These pieces were in process of being polished to perfect brightness by the butler, as I discovered on invading the pantry to use the telephone.

Mrs. John Jacob Astor, whose eloquent vocabulary won the title of the "Astorian dialect," was one of her friends and contemporaries, and Mrs. August Belmont, who was for many years, by right of personal grace and distinction and her husband's large fortune, the undisputed leader of New York in the latter years of the nineteenth century. These ladies wrote many letters, sentimental and fluent, were devoted to their families and friends, and had a high sense of the perfectibility of all such relationships.

Dr. Henry de Koven, my husband's father, was more distinguished in his appearance and manner than any American I ever saw. In his early youth he was sent to England to visit Sir William and Lady Farquhar, to whose house on a week-end visit came no less a person than Talleyrand, then ambassador to England. The young American was brought down from his bed to be exhibited to Talleyrand as a sample of what America could produce. He was related, through his grandmother, Margaret Winthrop, to many New York and Boston people who took themselves, and with justification, very seriously. He married Charlotte LeRoy, the only daughter of Jacob, who was a member of what was then the ruling family in New York. Mr. LeRoy drove the first four-in-hand which tooled along those brownstone avenues. He lived next the William Astor house on Lafayette Place, and his books and pictures, his silver and china, all testify to the taste of the day, a taste quite as beautiful as that which distinguishes the owners of the great fortunes of the present time, and perhaps more harmonious and classic.

My husband's mother was tall and imposing, by no means beautiful, but very witty and agreeable. After her marriage, she was given by her father one of the

Livingstone houses in Tivoli, but their residence was short in this lovely old house by the Hudson, for Dr. de Koven soon resigned his pastorate at the neighboring Redhook to become professor of homiletics in the theological seminary at Middletown, the home of his father and the residence of others of his family.

In Middletown, in fact, in a pillared house on its elm-shaded main street, my husband was born, and there his parents lived until 1870, when Dr. de Koven's health, broken by too many walks up the hill to the seminary, which overtaxed his delicate heart, was compelled to abandon his profession and leave America. Thus, from the age of eleven until twelve years later, when he alone returned to America, my husband lived in Europe. His father prepared him for Oxford, teaching him all the Latin necessary before he was fourteen. Then in an interval there was a year of music study at Stuttgart, for the boy who had already composed songs and shown distinct promise of his later talent. Another period with a tutor in England and four years at Oxford, where he took honors in history. Again Stuttgart, and then Florence, where Dr. de Koven eventually decided to live, after periods in Paris and Biarritz. In Florence, where Dr. de Koven had leased the Villa Camerata, my husband took his place in what was, during the year 1880 and later, a very agreeable center of European society, composed of the representatives of the great names of Florence, as well as French, English, and Dutch residents, such as the Comtesse de Talleyrand, the Duc de Dino, and Mme. D'oog Voorst. For the Comtesse de Talleyrand he used to lead cotillions, and frequently visited Mme. D'oog Voorst in her white-and-gold ballroom, at the usual appointed hour of midnight, to listen to her brilliant talk. He was then only twenty, but was highly appreciative of the remarkable woman who for so long held her court in the Italian city. His father saw no reason why his son should be dissatisfied with so agreeable a life, where as a member of the exclusive club, "The Union," he used to associate with the young Italians of that day. But he was restless for a more useful activity, and sailed for America and its opportunities for some sort of career. Landing in New York, he spent a summer at Newport with his aunt, Mrs. Dickey, there taking so successful a part in some amateur theatricals that he was offered immediately professional engagements as a comedian! The play was Pinero's "Amazons," and in the gymnasium scene my husband brought down the house by very successfully standing on his head.

This, however, was not his ambition, and as Judge Dickey offered him no employment, he came to Chicago, where his uncle, Mr. John de Koven, placed him in his bank at a salary of $25 a week, and so I met him.

In the brief interval of our wedding journey we visited Florence. The avenue of lime trees which then were thickly planted between the lodge and the gate of the Villa Camerata, seemed a road of mysterious ivy-wreathed darkness as we arrived one morning from the station. Within the courtyard, and assembled on the steps, were all the family, except Dr. de Koven himself, who was already very ill, and all the servants. My husband's mother clasped her recovered son in her arms, as the tears flowed from her eyes in silent emotion, too tender for words.

Nightingales sang in the grove near the villa. June was glorious in the rose garden and the purple hills surrounded us. On the brim of the hill cup, purple as porphyry, running over with flowers, the Villa Camerata looked up to Fiesole and down to the town. And from the cup rose an essence, like incense, from that fire of beauty which here blazed in its triumph, the expression of genius touched to inspiration by the holy spirit of art. And this incense, still potent, still living, breathed upon us with a sense of something almost sacred in those first weeks of our marriage. Something sacramental there was also in the blessing of that exquisite silver-haired gentleman, my husband's father, as he laid his hands on my head in farewell. It was indeed farewell, for only a few weeks later, on Mount Engelberg, his heart failed suddenly and he departed one morning to the higher mount of immortality. Mrs. de Koven died as suddenly, in the lonely villa, the next summer, so that if I had not gone to them immediately after my marriage I should never have known them. They were inexpressibly kind to me, interested also to see their new daughter-in-law, even a little curious, perhaps, for, as they had written, they had "never known any Western people." Mrs. de Koven was almost resentful that her son should be as "much in love" as she found him. But I like to remember that she most generously expressed her liking for her rival in her son's affections. They showed me, as they were well able, the wonders of Florence and introduced me to many of their friends.

94

Florence 1884

Reginald de Koven
AGED 7

I was taken to drive in the Cascine, a ceremony as sacred to the Florentine society of that day as the ocean drive in far-away Newport. I visited the gardens and villas. I saw the pictures. I met old Lady Orford in the garden of the Torrigiani villa, with her faded blond wig thickly powdered, and blazing jewels pinned on her black calico dress. But she was still a Walpole and was as poignantly witty as her long and varied reputation demanded. I went one evening to the high-ceilinged palace of the Marchesa Piccollelis and was kissed on both cheeks by that ancient heroine of a Polish romance, as I entered. The Duc de Dino was there and very gracious to the almost inarticulate young American bride, who could not speak French or Italian, but who could listen, in an unforgotten excitement, as her husband sang his own songs to his own accompaniment.

My mother had furnished us a sum with which to buy objects for her just completed town house; one of these which we bargained for delightedly in our first experience in shops of antiquities was a silver lamp, shaped as a cupid and shaded by butterfly wings. We brought it back in triumph to my mother, who sweetly gave it to us, so that that little god of love, with its unbroken wings, has been our household deity, standing on our dining room table during all the thirty-six years which were given us to live together.

At the port of New York, a letter, which told us that his father had died, was put in my husband's hands. No standard of breeding, no ideals of duty and conduct, were ever more clearly expressed and exemplified by any American gentleman than by my ever-to-be-remembered father-in-law. His relation with his wife, with whom he never ceased to enjoy endless conversations of mutual delight and interest, was itself a standard of all that a marriage of distinguished and intelligent people may and should be. His extreme distinction of bearing was famously caricatured in Lowell's *Biglow Papers*, where, as the attractive young curate who had married the New York heiress, he was entitled "The Reverend Cream Cheese."

"Poor Henry!" exclaimed Mrs. de Koven, when I rather audaciously communicated this hitherto unsuspected fact to them. "You are a very crushed cheese at present." And this remark, with its reference to his severe illness, so soon to close his life, was an example of her humor, which could save any situation capable of saving.

CHAPTER SEVEN

ON our return to America we went to my father's house in Lake Forest and there passed the quiet months of mourning. Life assumed a new and serious aspect. The years of girlhood gayety were over, and with the passing of the honeymoon of early marriage, questions of my husband's occupation presented themselves inevitably. No better solution of this problem was discovered than his entrance into my father's business. We passed the first winter of our marriage in an apartment in Chicago, and in the great wholesale house of the J. V. Farwell Company my husband wrestled, very unhappily, if the truth must be told, with the unsympathetic details of the dry-goods business, where my father had turned him loose—if I may use the expression — among silks and their mispronounced French names, among cottons and woolens, with no very definite position. I think my father was really at a loss to know what to do with this son-in-law of European education. And music, his beloved music, was always calling him. I have in my mind's eye a picture of my perplexed young husband, sunk in a deep blue armchair, who, at my question as to his profound despondency, announced that he was convinced he had done very wrong to heed his father's advice to give up music as a career. That talent will find some way of express-

97

ing itself, and will try all sorts of experiments, was shown by my husband's attempts to found a weekly paper. This little sheet was called *The Rambler.* Harry Smith, who afterwards was the librettist of "Robin Hood" and of many other successful comic operas, was coeditor. My husband contributed weekly short stories, some of them very witty, Harry Smith his well-turned *vers de société,* Albert Sterner the illustrations, and I myself several rather sentimental poems. But as the paper used most of the allowance my father had given us, and we could not pay the butcher's bill, *The Rambler* was, after a few months, compelled to cease its promising rambling.

Our first year of marriage was destined to show us the "seamy side of life." My husband passed the crisis of an exceedingly dangerous illness at the moment when our only child was born. It was therefore a very sad little family which left the apartment in Chicago to take refuge in the country house at Lake Forest. There, however, health returned to both of us, and there was great joy to my parents in their first grandchild.

In the autumn of 1885 we went to live with my father in the new house he had built in Chicago, near the wide avenue of many equally luxurious houses which overlooked Lake Michigan. This house, decorated by Tiffany of New York, was very large, with a well-furnished library, two drawing rooms hung with pictures, a beautiful dining room, and a ballroom on the third floor. There I was permitted to be a sort of delegated hostess at many dances, and was one of the committee of women, all older than myself, of the balls, called the "assemblies," where my husband, with Mr. Chatfield Taylor, later the husband of my younger and most lovely sister Rose, led the cotillions. Chicago had greatly changed since the days when its matrons wore their bonnets at receptions, and beautiful and perfectly dressed women graced assemblages of entirely cosmopolitan appearance.

I was selected at this time also to be the president of a society called the "Friday Club," where, after the delivery of the appointed essay on one or another subject of literary or political or sociological import, the members debated and argued with a great display of wit and intelligence, if at first with some disregard of parliamentary proceedings. This society of the younger women of Chicago was intended to exercise them in both the written and the spoken word, in imitation of an older society, "The Fortnightly," where their mothers had enjoyed the same privilege. These societies may cause a smile, for they suggest the efforts of young communities in the process of development, but the smiles of all visitors to the meetings of both the older and the younger societies turned from amusement into pleasure and admiration at the usually very able and competent discussions to which they listened. More than any country, ours is organized in many interlocking associations, for literary and civic improvement and expression, and thus are developed the standards of intelligence and political responsibility. Thus also feminine instruction in useful activity is carried on past the too brief school days.

There was also a class for the study of Browning

conducted by an enthusiastic, although rather long-haired teacher, the Reverend Floyd Jones. We found this study very stimulating and also very productive of conversation on the part of the pupils. One of our members had the opportunity of meeting the poet himself in London, and, in return for the ardent admiration she laid at his feet, received an opinion of American women. This opinion, which she repeated to the class on her return, was in fact very flattering. Browning declared that the American woman was the best type he had known. He commented particularly upon her simplicity, her independence, upon her intelligence and truthfulness and her lack of pretension.

My husband had always been sought for in amateur theatricals since his success at Newport, and persuaded me, during the winter of 1886, to join him in a very ambitious season of plays produced by an amateur manager with professional associations. In one week the little company actually performed three plays, "Poor Pillicoddy," "The Rivals," and "Caste." In the second my husband played Joe Jefferson's part of Bob Acres with great success, while I struggled with the sentimental rôle of Lydia Languish. As the retired grocer in "Caste" my husband was so greasy and unctuous, so completely the grocer, that I could with difficulty keep my face in the little rôle I played by his side. The photograph of myself in Lydia Languish's red-velvet hat with its white ostrich plumes is a reminder of those days when nothing was too arduous for our enthusiasm.

There was also a women's Luncheon Society, a very

restricted one of eight members, of which I was a member and the youngest.

Mrs. Potter Palmer was the organizer of this club. She was half French, half Southern by birth, luxurious in her tastes, ambitious, kindly and rather formal in manner. Her great house with its fantastic towered architecture on the Lake Shore Drive was our usual place of meeting. In later years she became a noted collector of beautiful furniture, pictures, and porcelains, and even in those days had filled her salons with modern pictures by Monet and his school. Her husband had an adoring and somewhat terrified admiration for his beautiful and ambitious young wife. The testimony of his admiration, as expressed in his remarkable will, was unique as far as my knowledge extends of such documents. It gave her not only absolute control of his great fortune, but assigned a generous sum to his successor in case his wife should remarry. When I knew Mrs. Palmer first in those early days in Chicago she was almost a faultless example of Southern beauty, with a skin as white as a jasmine flower, dark hair, and romantic dark eyes. She was, however, less romantic than anyone I ever knew, and conducted her life with a practical ability undeflected by any temperamental disturbances, quite satisfied with her fortunate lot. I once heard her comment upon the unforgivable folly of the marriage of a beautiful friend to a man without fortune as if it belonged to the category of moral delinquencies.

Another member of this class of eight was Mrs. Dexter. She was life-loving, graceful and blond, with a step as buoyant as a nymph over spring pastures. Mrs. Caton, another member, was also overflowing with health and vitality and exceedingly handsome. The latter's sister, Mrs. Eddy, less exuberant, but exquisitely finished and graceful, was also of this club. Mrs. Prettyman, Lady Curzon's cousin, and Maude Howe Elliott, then in the early years of her beauty, made a delightful and decorative company at this long-abandoned lunch table. I have met many women in many cities and countries since those days in Chicago, but never knew any so simply and happily satisfied with life. Our conversation was of books, of ideals, rarely of personalities, except historical, and we discussed them with that simple confidence in our own opinions which has furnished the type of conversation found to be singularly harmonious with that of wider experience. Mrs. Palmer, after a tour of the world and its capitals, informed me that she preferred "her Chicago women" to any she had met in Europe. Mrs. Caton, later Mrs. Marshall Field, is still a very notable hostess in Washington. Mrs. Dexter, after her husband's death, was long a popular Boston resident among her husband's relatives, and Mrs. Maude Howe Elliott's very agreeable books of travel and reminiscence have enlightened many readers during the years which succeeded her residence in Chicago.

Mrs. Prettyman, born Jenny Remington, I saw in her youth, during an exciting week at New Haven, where I went to attend a certain dance called "the Junior Promenade" to which my cousin John Farwell had bidden me. Like Marguerite or Elaine she seemed to me,

Left to right: Mr. LeRoy de Koven, Mr. C. R. S. de Koven, Mrs. LeRoy
de Koven, Master Louis de Koven, Mrs. Reginald de Koven, Mr. Reginald
de Koven.

FLORENCE, JUNE 1884

as, clad in white, with a silver girdle, I saw her stepping demurely, with downcast eyes, beneath the New Haven elms. Many titles had been offered her during her travels with her mother (as we were told), handed in to them at the breakfast table. But she loved her painter whose gifts were not destined to bring the fortune which took her cousin to such high places and she was weary a little during those years in Chicago with household cares.

Her mother and Mrs. Leiter, born Carver, of an old Charleston family, were both beautiful in their youth, and the pure line of brow, the lovely blue eyes of these Southern ladies, were the inheritance of their daughters.

A word about Mrs. Leiter and her famous vocabulary might be pertinent. No vulgarian was this gracious and ambitious Southern woman, but a perfect reincarnation of that fantastic gentlewoman, Mrs. Malaprop. Long before she went to live in Washington she received in Chicago with every luxurious appointment of house and table. She was distinctly and most amusingly possessed of illusions of grandeur brought by many another Southern woman to the North. These illusions were put into efficient practice in the education of her beautiful daughters, a preparation for the careers which awaited them and which not only their mother, but the daughters themselves, expected and intended to realize. Did the illusion of grandeur always haunt the beautiful head of Mary Leiter, turning, a little fantastically, to pretension on the viceregal throne of India? Perhaps, for illness always releases inherited complexes, but the vision of Mrs. Leiter found its fulfillment, winged as it was by the arrows of great fortune, in the persons of her children. As for Mrs. Leiter's inhibition in her "parts of speech" so similar to that of Mrs. Malaprop, it was the delight of her contemporaries and a contribution to the "gayety of nations." "Isn't it dreadful the way those Spaniards are galooting the villages?" was one of her famous remarks about the Cuban war. A strategic talent distinctly constructive and probably Jewish assisted her daughter in her first invasion of London society, where ultra sensitiveness would have been an insurmountable handicap. But from her early nursery days, with a very able English governess, Mary Leiter knew just what she wanted.

Of such elements, of such predestined world figures, Chicago society of the years from 1880 to 1890 was composed. Mrs. Robert McCormick, later ambassadress to Austria and France, and her sister Mrs. Patterson, were daughters of the editor of the greatest journal of the West, the Chicago *Tribune,* and were very dominating, worldly wise and amusing. The three daughters of the New England Mr. Houghtaling, each more beautiful than the other, were not only exceedingly ornamental, but had a gay and irrepressible wit. Mrs. Griswold, the second daughter, has illustrated these qualities for many years in New York.

Around these feminine representatives of the mid-Western city were the able men who were making its remarkable history. Charles Dudley Warner, after a sojourn in Chicago, while its notable men were still living, declared that it possessed the best society in America. Miss Ethel Arnold, far more perceptive of the *nuances* and *provenance* of American standards and distinctions than her sister Mrs. Humphry Ward, told me that the society she had seen in Chicago was better, more characteristic, and at the same time more like that she had known in Europe than any she had seen in our country. When the poet and humorist, Eugene Field, met Mrs. Ward in London and informed her that he came from Chicago, she exclaimed:

"That is an Indian name. Do tell me about the customs of the tribes who inhabit the region."

"I am sorry I cannot inform you, madam," he replied, "for when I was caught I was living in a tree."

If I might venture my own opinion, based on an experience of Washington, New York, Boston, Philadelphia, and of Chicago itself, regarding Miss Arnold's flattering praise of the society of my native city, I should say that this judgment arose from the following reasons: Chicago (as I have already said) was founded and inhabited by New England people, who, like all colonists, represented the most vigorous elements of their origin. These vigorous people were permitted to develop away from the restricting conditions of the older centers, and thus attained the best results of their capabilities. They were a part of a community of prevailing and growing prosperity, willing and able to contribute to its happy and fortunate conditions, with no inherited prejudices or standards other than those of high and strict rules of conduct and character brought from Puritan New England. There were no divorces and no scandals in the Chicago of my youth and early marriage, and there was no sign of the two most depressing and restricting social vices, which are only too prevailingly present in all of the Eastern cities—snobbishness and love of money. Personal character and personal charm were quickly appreciated and given full opportunity.

Those who have left their birthplace to take their part in the life of New York and other Eastern cities have invariably been able to take their part with unusual address and ability, due to this early association with what are in fact the correct standards of life and character. An unusually quick recognition of the value of all elements of education and of civic development has always characterized Chicago. The first American orchestra was founded in Chicago, and remains to this day a highly finished body of musicians. The University of Chicago has the most brilliant instructors and scientific investigators in America. More successful painters and students of music have been developed in Chicago than in any other American city, and its opera house has taken its place beside that of New York. The Dawes Plan, which is the present hope of Europe, originated in the brain of a Chicago man.

Of the important men who were playing their part in the growth of Chicago I saw little except at the "Dancing Class," for they were too much absorbed in business. Mr. Mac Veagh and his wife were, as always, very kind to me, and I was a frequent visitor at their house on the Lake Shore Drive. Here, as in old days, I met the visiting strangers of distinction who were always sent to their care. Dinners were infrequent among the younger people, who met for the most part at the several series of dances, and, if it must be confessed, we women met very often at what I believe is an American institution, the women's luncheon party. That I became accustomed to the habit of very earnest conversation in these assemblies was perhaps too evident, as I concluded when at my first meeting with Henry James in London he observed that I "made him think of a luncheon party."

It was a reproach which I considered to be nothing less than national, but, if a reproach, it is also a misfortune that American women should be forced to exercise their conversational talent for one another's benefit. American husbands, as is well known, give an unequaled liberty, an enviable confidence and a chivalrous admiration to their wives—everything, in fact, except their comradeship. The attitude of American men to their wives is, however, the best development of our national life. They expect and receive loyal adaptation to the necessities of their careers in business or politics. They differentiate always between this submission and the subservience too often imposed upon European women. They leave to their wives the conduct of the house and the control of children, and if they abandon them too frequently to their own devices it is the inevitable result of their absorption in their business ambitions and occupations. Inherited fortunes are not the rule, even in these later years, in our country, and self-made men have little time for easy and enviable relaxation in mutually shared sports and pleasures. Country life is, however, the preference of the younger generation, and there is promise of other times and more agreeable customs.

At this point in my memories and reflections I wish to add my opinion to those so many times expressed regarding the differences and misunderstandings which exist between the English of England and the English of America. It is my conviction that they are unalterable. From the earliest Colonial days they were so clearly manifested that the subject was considered worthy of an analytical interlude by Parkman in his *History of Canada* during the early period of English occupation. The unaccountable contempt shown by the English for the Colonists, who were born in England itself and were close blood relations, was a mystery to the historian, as it has been to the generations of succeeding Americans. Washington himself was treated with such cruel insolence while he was in Braddock's ill-fated army that he decided to leave the king's service. This singular undervaluation of their own kin, with the conviction that the cowardly yokels they called "Yankees" would never be able or willing to fight for their independence, was one of the causes of the dilatory mismanagement of the American war. If Lord George Germaine had not left the ill-written orders for the juncture of Carlton's troops with those of Burgoyne in a pigeonhole when he went off for his week-end in the country, Burgoyne's capture, with that of his whole army, would never have made that curious page of history. The conduct of a campaign across an ocean, when there was, as yet, no telegraph, was in itself an example of the English fidelity to routine which has in later years been tragically repeated.

The German brutality, as shown in the burnings and violations of the Hessian mercenaries, inflicted upon patriot and tory farmers alike, was, as is well known, the cause of the recovered determination of the Colonists to continue the war, when the lists of the signers to the amnesty proposals of the English general were nearly long enough to bring it to a conclusion. So English carelessness and German brutality won for us the War of Independence quite as truly as the assistance of the French.

English lack of imagination, English misunderstanding of their American cousins, still persist, and in these later years, when the American stock begins to be overbalanced if not diluted by foreign immigration, the hope of a better understanding grows less. Although the original mixture of the English, French, and Dutch people who made the admirable type of American has not been diluted or greatly altered in essentials of conduct or character, the millions who flood our country *are* intermarrying and are making a new people whose type it is impossible to visualize.

The Americans, after winning their national independence, were immediately conscious of this independence and at once assumed an attitude far different from that of the Colonials, who are still British subjects. Since that time they have not possessed or admitted one iota of provincial inferiority. For this reason they resent the usual appellation of "The States," applied to our country as a persistent suggestion of its provincial character. This attitude of independence is increased by the absence of recognized castes or social divisions. The servility of those who submit to be considered middle or lower classes does not exist in America, or the hypocrisy which often accompanies it. This, as Lord Bryce quite correctly observed, is the principal cause of the happiness which he admitted to exist in our country to a greater degree than in any other. King Edward, with that kindly and unprejudiced perception for which he was so justly loved, understood that there were American gentlemen and gentlewomen and greatly liked them. The tuning-fork of instinct must give back the answering note in any society, with or without titles. In our country it is the only test and basis of friendship. Yet the old insult that good breeding is confined to exceptional individuals is repeated and re-repeated *ad nauseam-ad desperandum*. Good blood with its commanding rule of gentle behavior and gentle thoughts is very persistent. It persists through generations, through intervening years of poverty and struggle. Sensitiveness and delicate feeling are the titles of native nobility, and if from the European angle it too frequently seems to turn to touchiness and to needless explanation, it is the inevitable result of nearly two centuries of persistent undervaluation.

A deplorable lack of attention to agreeable accent and speech, a curious contagion of bad intonation, spreads over our country and causes many, whose character and instincts are beyond criticism, to be hopelessly misunderstood. A gentlewoman who speaks with an accent which represents the social scale of a cockney must expect to be misjudged and probably avoided when she goes on her travels. Yet this same gentlewoman has a pride which expects to return favors, who never bargains or calculates the advantages of friendship and has not learned to be insolent. This lesson is the fruit of a decadent aristocracy. Merit first, then privilege, then vain pretension are the descending steps of a social order now at the point of disappearance. Every period in social development has its dominating idea. The idea of the present period is evidently "the greatest good for the greatest number." In America this idea is marching toward realization. If in the enormous "melting pot" (to use an overworked word) of our nation a new and vigorous language develops with startling disharmonies of freshly coined words, if manners, the manners of enriched Jews, Irish, Russians, Germans, and Scandanavians, are crude and jarring to every sensibility, liberty and free opportunity for ambition are raising the standard of human happiness and lifting ignorance and inexperience to ever higher levels of progress. Upon the original Anglo-Americans and their descendants has devolved the task of assimilating the undeveloped millions who come from the farms and cottages of Europe. It is for them to teach the standard of the gentleman, who "never willingly gives pain to another."

Metaphor is always approximate and generalities are like armies with banners, challenging as many opposing exceptions. Yet nature, which decrees that youth should be plastic and age crystallized, imposing this inevitable progress upon all forms of life, gave me, in a pine forest near Nuremberg, an example of the history of nations. This forest, seen when I was myself in my impressionable youth, seemed to me a type of the English people. Roots of iron supported long serried shafts of denuded giants, except for sky-touching branches, delicate and triumphantly waving, almost out of sight. Fixed opinions and standards in the English seemed to me to resemble the roots of these pine trees. Denuded boles in a sunless darkness, the insular isolation of the middle classes and their ignorance. High waving branches, the gay courage and chivalry which are the ultimate crown and development of the English *noblesse*. The progress of nature is never reversive, thus instinctive comprehension of other and younger races is not to be expected from the English, and argument or explanation is as futile as the hope that age will retrace the long road to childhood. The Round Table still exists in our mother country, where there are prelates, great gentlemen and ladies, scholars and saints of every degree, but that an American, not superior, but such as we ourselves consider to be no more than typical, should find himself *orienté* only with the saints and the knights, the survivals and perfected examples of high spiritual preceptions, is a fact of considerable significance. With them contact is both illuminating and merciful, rich in sympathy and understanding. Such is not the experience either with those of the untraveled middle classes or with those who assume that privilege permits unkindness. The vessel of steel recks not of the ruin its undented contact inflicts upon a *pâte* of fine porcelain, of perfect or imperfect polish. To return in kind the blows to sensibility entails too great a sacrifice, no less than a profound alteration of character in the loss of this same sensibility. The price is too great to pay even for victory. No expression of the fidelity of English friendship, no kindness or hospitality to those who have been received as exceptional Americans, reverses the prevailing and too generally contemptuous English opinion. Castes and race differences are doubtless less determining in this period of liquidation, of rapid transition, and the ascendency of a great people in the vanguard of the march of human development does begin to impose its mass and its vigor upon Europe. Sensitiveness and idealism may have their apparent weaknesses, but they also have their perceptions. Steel, although merciless in contact, may be tenacious, and that tenacity often becomes great and unbreakable loyalty. If sensitiveness perceives this, idealism hopes for the widest expression of this loyalty in an Anglo-American friendship. Of this there have already been many historical examples.

No American ever forgets Manila Bay, or the orders, issued from the English Embassy in Washington, at the beginning of our war with Spain, which scattered the nearly completed combination of the other Chancelleries of Europe against us. English justice, English standards of friendship, English simplicity and lack of affectation, are as well known to us as English history and English literature, and if misunderstanding of us, who are inheritors of all these glories, must persist, that inheritance is none the less our own and the very essence of our character and of our motives of thought and action.

Will the American form of civilization, up to this time a derivation of the English in both standards of justice and in customs, succeed in amalgamating the hordes of unrevolved units of the *genus homo?* The task of the leaders and teachers, born Anglo-Americans, is enormously greater than that which was accomplished in England when its differing races were being welded into a nation. But the Anglo-Saxon strain has a leavening quality whose power is still predominant. Upon the failure or success of this leavening influence awaits the solution of the staggering problem and the hope of the world.

The American wing of the Metropolitan Museum in New York, with its transferred rooms from early Colonial houses, with their furniture, silver, brocaded dresses and India linens of fine embroidery, is an object lesson to all visitors, of the continued tastes and customs which the English Colonists brought overseas. English gentlefolk lived as became them and were not altered by the voyage to America.

The Atlantic coast towns of Salem, Ipswich, Newburyport and Portsmouth, preserved like butterflies in amber, are examples of purest Georgian architecture, purer, indeed, according to an exchange Oxford professor, than any remaining in England itself. Even Chateaubriand with his fantastic tales of imaginary Indian maidens has recorded that the little cities of Baltimore and Annapolis differed in no way from cities of the same size in England. As for the gallant company of young French noblemen who came to help us, they could and did forget Versailles and even the queen in her beauty, to lay their hearts and fortunes at the feet of the wild-rose beauty and the unassailable dignity of the Puritan maiden.

Like a deep diapason, in his hymn of praise of America in its idyllic period, is De Tocqueville's repeated Cassandra warning of the "resistless march of democracy." In that march, dignities and titles and thrones have been swept away, for it is not a peaceful progress; it proceeds like a forest fire with destruction. In America there has been nothing old to destroy and its new and vigorous growth is with the present and the future.

The persistent idealism of our country, born of that aristocracy of good instinct which is the glory of nature's nobility, is the molding, inspiring force which makes America the training place for the ignorant aspiring multitudes who flock to its shores and rapidly develop in its atmosphere of freedom. The rapidity with which this influence is absorbed is in truth very remarkable. Among the foreign children there is seen a plastic facility, and an eager ambition, to take a self-respecting part in the great Republic. The sight of these children in the public schools of our country and the enthusiasm of their participation in the address to the flag is a spectacle which brings to any visitor astonishment, hope, and emotion.

So, almost as if the hand of God were moving over the face of the waters, the amazing metamorphosis takes place, and in spite of crudeness and inharmonies manifold and inevitable, the human race in all its varieties is mounting the hill of progress under the ægis of the justice and the benefits inherent in our form of government.

The apparent divergencies in their harmony with recognized standards of manners and speech between American men and American women is the universal comment of Europeans. This divergency is, however, only apparent. The college boy when he emerges from his studies differs in no unlovely detail from his sister, but his fate is to plunge at once into the maelstrom of "business." There he is forced to associate with the half-cooked but not half-vitalized newcomer and rival by way of the steerage. Refinements of speech and manner become disadvantages and are attributed to affectation. The struggle for success, even in a land of equal opportunity, is fierce and keen, and all unnecessary handicaps, as in a running race, must be cast aside. Too little leisure is left for the cultivation of tastes or talents in this breathless competition, and lessons of gentle homes and happy college years are too often forgotten. Standards and habits of business and business only are stimulating to manly muscle, but not to the smoothness of the exterior. Certain undesirable habits of mind born of the too keenly played game also develop, so that the strange anomaly sometimes appears of American men who are idealistic in private life, abounding in charity, and rather less than ethical in business. That there should be a different standard of honor in private and business relations is clearly regrettable. Generosity to a foe in business who is striving to make the best of all bargains is not, perhaps, to be expected.

But the character of unbargaining, uncalculating idealism in private and international affairs should leaven the whole lump of American life. The psychology of a game played to the limit and sometimes beyond it is very easy to understand, but not easy to counteract. When getting the best of a bargain becomes a commonplace and then a rule of business, it is not easy to differentiate its ethical significance or to impose a more human and a broader standard. Leisure, that unattainable goal of the American man of business, would develop these broader and higher modes of thought. Idealism, however, burns with an undying flame. It blazes from the fantastic signs of Broadway, to the confusion of every transatlantic visitor, who wanders, half blinded, among the sights and sounds and the cloud-scaling towers of our amazing cities, quite unable to account for the character or the meaning of such manifestations of human activity. The Babbitts who make romances of real-estate activities, the insurance agents who at banquets use metaphors of crude poetic illustration, calling their triumphant company their "mother" and, indulging in every extravagance of loyalty to their life's enterprise, are all soldiers exulting in business, and, like the knights of the Middle Ages, go singing to their battles. And if architecture reflects the soul of a people, then indeed we may point to the last developed order, the skyscrapers, which upon the pylons of Egypt pile the towers of Giotto and fling a vertiginous pattern of illuminated, lacy architecture against the Western sky of this new empire of the people, who have at last, after centuries, come into their own.

117

CHAPTER EIGHT

"THE BEGUM"

IN the winter of 1886 my father was elected Senator, and it is my pride that he asked me to accompany him to Washington to see him take the oath of office. This ceremony I witnessed from a seat in the gallery and was immensely proud of the distinguished body of men to which he was admitted. He had been elected almost by acclamation by the Illinois Legislature, suddenly freed from the domination of Senator Logan, who was kept in the Senate by the extraordinary and most successful campaign methods of his wife, in the districts of southern Illinois. Senator Logan died at the end of the year 1885 and my father was chosen to fill his unexpired term. The romance of war distinction had placed this descendant of Indians (if one could assume this extraction from a face as black as the night and possessed of every Indian trait of physiognomy) in the political arena. No constructive political ability was his, as his record clearly shows, but his relations with the Illinois farmer members of the Springfield Legislature were most carefully nurtured and their numerical superiority over those of the north of Illinois was sufficient to delay the choice of my father for membership in the Senate during Logan's lifetime. The satisfaction of my father at finally attaining to what was for many years the greatly desired prize of all political ambition was

118

characteristically frank and happy. And this satisfaction was particularly keen because in his last term in Congress, President Harrison, with a deplorable lack of discrimination, had classed him with the admittedly corrupt leaders of other states and removed from his hands all the local appointments which had, by invariable party customs, been given to the congressional representative.

The incident pertaining to Harrison's refusal to nominate Mr. Campbell to the custom house of Chicago is worth recording. To my father's just indignation and astonishment, he found that the President had requested Mr. John Clark of Chicago, an entirely non-political resident, to select all the local appointees. This was a totally undeserved blow to the man who, since the early days of Chicago, had been its able and justly popular political leader. Mr. Campbell had been for years an active supporter of the Republican party in Chicago, and his selection for the proposed office was legitimate and justified. But President Harrison described him as a "corrupt politician" in the letter he wrote my father in which he declined to appoint him.

But when Mr. Harrison essayed to succeed himself as President, that carelessness of observation which had ignored the significance of my father's character and influence in Chicago betrayed him into selecting this same Campbell as the chairman of his campaign committee. Here then was an opportunity for revenge which was too excellent to be ignored. My father wrote to the editor of the *Washington Post* as follows:

Dear Sir:

I observe that Mr. Campbell of Chicago has been chosen as the chairman of the National Republican Campaign Committee by President Harrison. I would like to inquire whether this is the same Mr. Campbell whom Mr. Harrison refused to appoint as Collector of Customs of the Port of Chicago, on my recommendation, for the reason that he was a corrupt politician and unfit for office.

The withdrawal of the unlucky candidate's name as the result of this pertinent inquiry was naturally inevitable, and my father's contentment was seriously diminished by Mr. Campbell's deprivation of the important place of campaign manager.

The defeat of Harrison and the Republican party was an equally mixed satisfaction. Although my father was by no means lacking in that sense of humor which corrects both vanity and intolerance and adds to philosophy, and although he always enjoyed and often repeated a good story, he rarely invented them. But his experience with Harrison added an edge to his pen and also to his speech, as I was informed by that well-known Senator Platt who was for many years a power to reckon with in New York politics. I met him at dinner at the house of Mayor McClellan, and well remember his enjoyment in relating the story.

"Your father," he said, "had gone to the White House to protest against his deprivation of the Chicago appointments and was informed by the officer who stood at the door of the President's office that 'he could not be seen.'"

"What!" said your father. "Has he then grown so small that he is invisible?"

This reply, if my knowledge of my father's reluctance to "blow his own trumpet" may be trusted, could only have been repeated by the White House official who did not fail to appreciate it, as much as "Tom Platt" and in fact the whole of official Washington.

Harrison's attitude toward my father was not shared by President Cleveland, his predecessor and successor, and his request to my father to name for chief justice of the Supreme Court a man from Chicago was the remarkable expression of the Democratic President of his valuation of the leading Republican of Illinois. To this act of President Cleveland Judge Fuller owed his appointment.

During that visit to Washington to see my father enter the Senate, I went to a Diplomatic reception and there, among the many guests, was introduced to President Cleveland and his wife. It was her first appearance after her marriage and there was no dissenting note in the praise which her lovely youth, her grace, and her simplicity evoked from Diplomats and Americans alike. No act of his life was expressive of more wisdom than Cleveland's choice of this delightful and most intelligent woman. My sister and I were permitted to share an hour of her time a few years later, when she paid us the compliment of relating to us a very intimate and touching account of the President's emotion at his children's first lisping prayers at his knee. It is interesting to note that a late English book on "public life" in England and America includes a letter from Cleveland to a would-be profiteer of the city privileges in

Buffalo, when Cleveland was mayor of that city, as an example of fearless honesty in politics.

Another much later meeting with Mrs. Cleveland in the year 1918, when she was Mrs. Preston, revealed her desire to assist any honest endeavor. I had placed before her and her husband, who had himself been a college professor, the half-finished manuscript of a little book on citizenship. Although unfinished, they gave me most intelligent encouragement in regard to this work, and through Mrs. Preston's influence I was able to do some work under Professor McElroy of the Security League. This work was, as Mrs. Preston had foreseen, the intermediate step to a favorable introduction to the New York Board of Education. The work I had done was an investigation of the patriotic activities of the New York public schools during the war, and to consider my report Prof. McElroy assembled certain public school principals and the Superintendent of the Board of Education. I was thus introduced to Dr. Tildsley, who not only approved of my manuscript, but presented it to the school-book experts of the City Board. The words of encouragement which I received from Mrs. Preston and her husband were confirmed by Dr. Tildsley's advisers, and I am not only glad to render to them my thanks for their appreciation, but to express my astonishment that the half-finished manuscript should have elicited so quick a valuation.

In Washington in 1886 Mrs. Cleveland and I were both young, and thoughts of Princeton University for her and of school books for me were not in our dreams. If the history of the ladies of the White House were to be written, it is my opinion that with Dolly Madison and Mrs. Roosevelt, Mrs. Cleveland would represent the best type of American womanhood in this place of dignity and publicity.

I spent only a few weeks among my old friends in Washington during that winter of 1886. I danced in quadrilles with lovely Mary Leiter in her mother's house and with equally lovely Adèle Grant. I talked as before of politics with politicians in the city of my childhood and girlhood, but an illness of my husband's recalled me to Chicago, and there was also at that time a promise of a new and important development in his life and career which demanded immediate attention.

Music as ever haunted his thoughts and engaged all his time away from the office of the J. V. Farwell Company. There was, in that year of 1886, no company which produced comic opera except that under the management of Colonel McCaull, who presented to the audience of the day only French and Viennese operas. My husband had vainly sought for a manager, when one day Colonel McCaull visited Chicago and came to my father's house at my husband's invitation. His leading actress and singer, the very brilliant Austrian called Mathilde Cottrelly, told me that after my doubtless naïve and probably amusing plea to him "to please put on my husband's opera, even if we did not really need to have him do it," he said: "I believe I will put on the opera. I would like to, because that young woman asked me." However this unusual plea might have evoked his fancy, he was not fanciful enough to forego a guaranty for part of the production, which fortunately we were able to furnish. The important, the all-important object was attained, for under the best, the only real manager of the time, this first opera of my husband was destined to be well performed.

Although a first attempt at writing a comic opera had been made by my husband, a doubtless very amateurish production called "Cupid, Hymen & Co.," which never saw the light, the comic opera produced by Col. McCaull was the first opera which deserved the name. It was called "The Begum," and the libretto, a burlesque and amusing story of an Indian princess and her admirers, was written by Harry Smith. It was produced in Philadelphia, in the winter of 1887, at the Philadelphia Opera House. This occasion was celebrated by the inhabitants of the Quaker City with much enthusiasm. Flags were hung from the boxes as appropriate decoration for this production of American comic opera. In the year 1845 a so-called comic opera was put on the stage for a brief period. But with "The Begum" it may be said that my husband scored the first success in this field and that he, in fact, actually initiated the epoch of light opera in America. "The Begum" was beautifully staged and the costumes quite magnificent. Mathilde Cottrelly was the Begum, and played the rôle with humor and her usual excellent singing. Marion Manola was the soprano, and there were no less than four exceedingly good comedians—De Wolf Hopper, de Angelis, Digby Bell, and Harry McDonough, each and all quite sufficient to fill the rôle of leading and sole comedian in many succeeding American productions. And this first venture succeeded. It played to good houses during the season and was financially re-munerative. Those first notices, which we saw at five o'clock the morning after the production, were favor-able, to our immense satisfaction, although some evening papers were not so encouraging to the young composer. But, on the whole, we had every reason to be content. The press was satisfied that an American should enter the field unoccupied up to that date by any but foreign competitors.

In Chicago, however, one reporter announced that he "would never give a good notice to a man who led ger-mans"—and my husband took the opportunity pub-licly to reply that Wagner and others had been equally guilty. The conductor of cotillions, then sometimes called "germans," had a difficult road to follow in demo-cratic America. One other reporter, who visited him in his office, was mollified by discovering some dust on my husband's high collar, which had aroused already much resentment on the part of his colleagues of the news-papers.

But there was a far more serious attempt to question the ability of the young musician. A cruelly false and deliberately altered report of an interview with a Ger-man musician called Seebeck, to whom my husband had given some copying, was issued, with the design of im-plying that this Seebeck had written the score of my husband's opera. Denials from Seebeck and apologies from the newspapers were powerless to arrest the course of the falsehood. A statement, published widely by my husband, offering to give up all his royalties to anyone who could prove Seebeck had written a note of his music, was of course unanswered and put an end to the virulent attack.

Although we had by this time begun to build our own home in Chicago, the success of "The Begum" gave great encouragement to my husband's desire to follow a musical career and eventually altered our lives.

CHAPTER NINE

ALTHOUGH my husband's studies at Stuttgart had enabled him to compose the score of "The Begum," he felt that he needed further instruction in orchestration and decided to follow the advice of Madame Cottrelly and go to Vienna to study with Richard Genet. The composer of "Nanon" was the *doyen* of the school of Viennese comic-opera composers, among whom Von Suppé, Millöcker and Strauss were pre-eminent, and they had all studied with this master of orchestration. We therefore left our little daughter in my mother's care and sailed for Europe in the spring of 1888.

We found with great difficulty an apartment in Vienna, for it was then likened to a potter's field, a place in which to bury strangers, as no place was provided in which they could live. The curiously arranged rooms, we discovered, were let and furnished by an unfortunate heroine of an early love tragedy which had turned her brain. They were situated in the short street called the Canova Gasse, near the Hotel Imperial, where we took all our meals except our morning chocolate, which was prepared by my black-eyed Austrian maid, Betty. This pleasant handmaiden's vocabulary I soon mastered, but no more, and I was always amused by her affectionate kiss on my hand with which she greeted every command of her young mistress. She and our poor little landlady used to call us the "happy pair," and who shall say that our youth, our occupation, our bits of song as we mounted the stairs from the courtyard, did not justify this title? But I was at first very lonely, for my absorbed husband did not hear any remark I addressed to him while he worked. I wept for three weeks at this unusual situation, and then decided that the German lessons I was taking were not sympathetic enough to engage my interest, and began to translate that masterpiece of Pierre Loti, "Le Pecheur d'Islande." I had no idea, as I proceeded with this occupation, that my translation would ever be published. It *was* published after my return to Chicago by A. C. McClure & Co. This was in 1889, and it still brings me royalties and, what was of far more importance, the approbation of my friend, Jules Cambon, who read it in Washington in 1899. I knew very little French when I attempted this translation, but my knowledge of Latin helped me, and a certain ear for the lilt of a phrase. The exercise in seeking English parallels to those beautiful descriptive sentences which Loti never surpassed was of very definite use to me in my later writings. It taught me, in fact, some French, but much more English.

We were very much alone in Vienna, undisturbed with our work, and far happier, I think, than we realized. We went occasionally to the Lichtenstein Palace, which our then *chargé d'affaires,* Mr. James Roosevelt, and his charming wife, the former Helen Astor, had taken for the summer at Weidlingau. There we used to watch a tennis game, remarkable enough, indeed, for one of the players was the Cardinal Merry del Val, then a young novitiate, who in his long soutane, looked like a pictured Saint Sebastian. We used also to dine at Lavin's, then the correspondent of the London *Times,* and there saw very frequently an old music master, so poor that he was asked to take his share of the coffee and bonbons at the end of dinner. Of him I was persuaded, because he was so sadly in need, to take singing lessons. Often enough I have been asked if I was "musical" by interested strangers on first acquaintance. My reply has often been the relation of the following incident.

To his weekly conferences with Genet my husband was accustomed to bring original compositions, and one of these, which in twenty minutes I had heard him compose, was the song "Oh, Promise Me." A few days after he had written it we were asked to dine at the house of Baron d'Anethan and his wife. He was the son of the then Premier of Belgium, and his wife the sister of Rider Haggard. They had been ordered to Brazil, and it occurred to me that I could safely try my newly acquired vocal skill upon these departing diplomats. I therefore took a book of songs under my arm, and was duly asked to sing. Their comments were only too significant of my capacity, being confined strictly to compliments about the song. My husband then followed and sang to his own accompaniment (he had studied the piano professionally, and always had a particularly beautiful touch) this recently composed "Oh, Promise Me." Our hosts were far too intelligent to fail to recognize the talent of the young musician, too quick in judgment and in musical taste to fail to appreciate the song which has sold in its millions, and is now, between Mendelssohn's and Wagner's wedding marches, used as an obligato during the marriage ceremony itself all over our country. It was not surprising that I closed my book of songs and decided that there could never be any musical rivalry in our family. The study of music went on all summer, and at the end of that time the score of the opera composed to another of Harry Smith's librettos, and called "Don Quixote," was performed by a famous orchestra in Vienna, one morning in an empty theater. Genet, my husband, and myself were the only audience. I took my place behind a pillar in the gallery, saying to myself, "In a few moments I shall know whether my husband really has a career." In a few moments I knew, for the enormous advance in orchestration, united to the remarkable lyric gift which my husband possessed, was evidence enough to convince his anxious young wife, as she awaited the sounds which announced the future. Genet was not only satisfied with his great diligence and progress, but promised the career which was fortunately destined to be his.

Those days of exile, for we were lonely except for each other, laid the foundation for my husband's success, and were, perhaps, the happiest of all our lives. We were young, we had promise and absorbing work, and each other's help and companionship. Over forty years have gone by since that summer when my husband was preparing himself for his future usefulness, and now, with his life work finished and the earthly scroll of our happiness rolled up forever, I recall so vividly his fair head as he bent over the keys, hear the melodies which flowed so easily from his beautiful hands, "Ah! long, long ago, long ago—"

We left Vienna and the summer solitude of its strange streets and closed houses in the autumn of 1888. We had, however, heard opera, under Richter's incomparable direction; we had visited very often the Café Ronacher; we had seen with interest at the Hotel Imperial, where we had dined and lunched all the summer, a group of Austrian officers, all at one table, very smart and good-looking, of whose names we were quite ignorant. But we saw them one day rise to their feet in great excitement, to greet an exquisite young creature, whose camellia white skin, whose dark eyes in her round pretty face, we recognized as belonging to the Baroness Vetsera; she was to meet her mysterious tragic fate only a few months later.

CHAPTER TEN

THE long journey back to America was accomplished with as little delay as possible. My husband, on returning to Chicago, continued for one winter more to fill his secretarial post with my father's Texas company. For that winter only we occupied our own house in Chicago. With the preference I have always had for sixteenth-century English architecture it was built with some originality on a twenty-five-foot lot, with the entrance floor designed as a high-ceilinged hall, with a deep fireplace, and an imitation tapestry. This was all we could afford in those days, but the window on the street had diamond-paned heraldic glass, and in the paneled dining room with steps leading up from the hall, portraits were set, and the wall with the door opening on the landing was also glazed and illuminated. On the second floor was a library, also paneled, and a blue-and-pink French drawing room. Here, to this house at 25 Bellevue Place, we began to invite the various actors and actresses who played in Chicago, such as the Kendals, Wilson Barrett, and Francis Wilson. "Don Quixote" was the first of my husband's operas to be performed by that famous Boston company, first called "The Boston Ideals," and afterward "The Bostonians." This company was composed of a number of church-choir singers who first produced such simple

132

lyric operas as "Martha," "Fatinitza," and "The Bohemian Girl." Barnaby was the comedian, Eugene Cowles the bass, McDonald the baritone and his wife the soprano, Jessie Bartlett Davis the contralto, Frothingham also a comedian, and Tom Karl the tenor. They were all stars in their several ways, the company most harmonious, and it was indeed fortunate that my husband, in writing "Robin Hood" to suit them, had such excellent actors and singers to fill every part.

Their existence as a company was uniquely long and successful in the history of America, and their memory is a very happy one to all who heard them and to all the writers and composers who were fortunate enough to intrust their works to their able performance. "Don Quixote" was moderately successful, as the music my husband had written in Vienna was beautifully tuneful and showed his new and from that time excellent command of the orchestra. But the libretto hardly realized the possibilities of the subject, and it remained for the next work of Reginald de Koven and Harry Smith to afford the company their best opportunity of success and to demonstrate their own combined talents. This opera—"Robin Hood"—was composed during the winter of 1888-89, in exactly three months. It was produced in the spring in Chicago, for a trial season of only two weeks; the production, a very provisional one, made up of old costumes and scenery, cost exactly $150. But as I found my way, in the utmost excitement, through the cellar of the theater, up to the wings after the performance, to find my husband, I was sure that it was not only a success, but a very brilliant and decisive "hit."

At this long distance of time which has elapsed, after the thirty-seven years that it has occupied the stage, I can best quote the editorial comment in the New York *Times* which appeared after my husband's death. This editorial contained the opinion that his operas should not be compared to Sullivan's, for the reason that his music was quite his own, and original in its fluent melody, and that the best parallel to "Robin Hood," with its pastoral, open-air atmosphere, was "As You Like It."

As I listen, in my mind's ear, to those merry tunes, as I recall the gems of pure melody, one after the other, which have for so long been the property of the American people, as I reflect that many of the numbers have sold separately into their millions, and that each without exception was sufficiently popular to make a success of any comic opera, I think, with a joy which is more than half grief, that the heart and mind from which they flowed must have been very happy.

Like a little boy whistling in the morning is this "Robin Hood" music. The crest of the wave—the best and most youthfully spontaneous expression of my husband's talent it undoubtedly is—and it has always been so considered. In the forty-one productions which succeeded this opera he wrote music quite as melodic, and often more mature, but for freshness and gayety, and for uninterrupted flow of happy inspiration, "Robin Hood" is unquestionably pre-eminent. The libretto also has always been thought the best his collaborator ever wrote. Harry Smith had a far finer literary quality than has been assigned to him. Deeply read in

English literature, as his present occupation of magazine writer and bookseller of rare editions proves him to be, his lyrics were often of a very charming and distinguished character, and often failed of due appreciation on account of the "comic medium" in which they were embodied. The theme of "Robin Hood" was very sympathetic to his fancy, and the careful adaptation of the rôles to the members of the excellent company who were to perform them produced an even superiority, in each and every case. Barnaby's Sheriff of Nottingham, a rôle he performed for over twenty years, will be remembered as the perfection of light and not over-emphasized comedy. McDonald as Scarlett, was the ideal of a handsome highwayman, with his six feet of manhood, clad in his brown boots and green jerkin, and his singing of "Brown October Ale," a model of ringing baritone. And Jessie Davis, as she stood beside him, also in brown boots and green jerkin, how boldly lovely she was, and what a couple they made against the green forest! Her singing of "Oh, Promise Me," which was introduced into the score of the opera, was famous for many years, and quite properly. Her voice was a truly splendid contralto, never so thrilling as in this song which she took an octave lower than it was written. She so loved it that she almost persuaded herself that she had written it herself, and directed that a copy of its adored melody should be buried in her coffin. Then there was Eugene Cowles, the bass, whose rendering of the Armorer's Song was quite as remarkable and as long remembered. Frothingham, the Friar, was an "unctuous" comedian, the last to survive of all this

135

famous company. Long after the passing of his comrades, "Robin Hood" was revived in the year 1908 at the New Amsterdam Theatre in New York with a remarkable company composed of many singers of the Metropolitan Opera. The production, with such singers, was necessarily very expensive, and only justified from the financial point of view of the managers by the great enthusiasm of the public, a new public of the younger people, who had never heard in New York the famous opera. For three months the theater was crowded, and the venture was not only successful, but quite unique for its singers and its stage settings and costumes, in the history of comic opera. Frothingham, the sole survivor of the old company, was called to the front of the stage on the first night of this revival, and broke into uncontrollable tears at the applause, which filled the theater, and at all those unforgettable memories of the silent singers who had been his companions for so many years.

During our last winter in Chicago, in the year 1889, I was also busy, having been encouraged in my budding literary ambitions by the success of my translation of Le Pecheur d'Islande. Very early in my own very humble career as a writer I had composed an article about Ireland, the first of the countries I had visited when on the family tour. My father, always anxious to encourage his children and as invariably kind to all poor and struggling people, had made the acquaintance of a certain Mrs. Starrett, wife of an impecunious clergyman, who was vainly trying to make a success of a monthly called *The Western Magazine*. He used fre-

My Father with the First Grandchild
CHICAGO, 1888

quently to talk to this valiant lady on the train which took him daily from Lake Forest to Chicago, and he proposed to furnish a small honorarium which she was to give me for an article. With pride, therefore, I wrote the article filled with the most innocent platitudes about Blarney Castle and the Lakes of Killarney, and was duly presented with twenty-five dollars. "What shall I do with this money," I asked myself, "the first I ever earned?" A present for my father, of course, was my decision. Thus he was the immediate owner of an inkstand for the exact sum he had given Mrs. Starrett. I keep it yet, that ugly inkstand, with thoughts and memories as beautiful as any which glorifies the *gage d'amour* of the faithfulest lover.

But from this small beginning some results did follow. The editor of the Chicago *Record,* then one of the leading journals, was about to start an evening paper—the *Post,* and having unaccountably seen the article on Ireland, and reflecting, as he told me, that "that young woman did not have to write," he asked me to conduct the literary page in his new paper. Thus, to my great pride and interest, I found myself most pleasantly employed, during that last winter in Chicago, in writing reviews of contemporary novels and other publications, in regard to which I am sure my judgments were less than valuable. Another curious development followed in the train of the article on Ireland. Mrs. Abbott, of Salem, the widow of a Bostonian who had conducted a mercantile business in Calcutta, spent most of that winter with us in our house in Chicago. She was far more capable of conducting the literary page in the *Evening Post* than I was, and when I left Chicago I recommended to the editor that she should take my place. Not only did she do this, but in the office met Peter Dunne, then editorial writer on the *Record,* published from the same office, and Peter Dunne, after a long friendship with this brilliant friend of mine, married her daughter. The most sparkling conversations which it has ever been my privilege to hear were those I listened to in her little apartment, between Mary Abbott and Peter Dunne. There I used often to stop during my return visits to Chicago, after we had left it, and often enough those conversations were interrupted, because, as Peter would reluctantly announce, he had to "go and write that Dooley rot." That *rot* was the sum of his improvisations on his conversation with one Hennessey, who presided at a too popular saloon. Herbert Stone, the son of Melville, the editor of a Chicago journal, recognized the value of these commentaries, and with some difficulty dug them out of the files and published them, and so Peter Dunne, the beloved Dooley, awoke one morning, to find himself famous.

As for Margaret's marriage to Peter Dunne, the Irishman, I have often declared to them that it never would have happened if I had not written that article on Blarney Castle which took me, and later my successor, Margaret's mother, into the office of that Chicago journal.

Peter Dunne's famous wit was and is companioned by a very wide knowledge of men and affairs which makes him a brilliant editorial writer. His sudden accession to fame was accompanied by as sudden an increase in knowledge which genius so often seems to acquire, as from the atmosphere, without visible means of communication. This phenomenon, really psychic, I have witnessed in other greatly gifted men of my acquaintance. It is the result, as I believe, of their endowment of a larger share of that mysterious section of our being which is called the subconscious mind, than is possessed by ordinary men. Thus gifted, through the open door of this inner being, the reservoir of knowledge existing about us pours into their minds a never ceasing increment of intuition. And this permeability to the thought waves by which we are surrounded renders these highly endowed beings immediately sympathetic to the character and the thoughts of all with whom they come in contact, so that they wield a great influence over men and women alike.

Peter Dunne of "The Interpreter's House" was indeed possessed of a wisdom born of this clairvoyant gift. So was Roosevelt, of whom his son-in-law said that he knew by some prophetic insight the future. He was in touch with the mass instincts of the people, and had on many an occasion shown a wisdom and foresight of which he could not trace the source.

So was William J. Bryan, with far inferior mental gifts, and so was and is Paderewski, the arch-interpreter of music, whose control of his audiences, who respond telepathically to his powerful personality, is famous.

That Bryan's control of his audiences was also due to this permeability to thought waves was singularly and amusingly illustrated in the following incident. I was making the journey from New York to Chicago some years ago and perceived "the golden-tongued" orator in a seat facing me, and as I recognized him I was impressed with the alteration from the pictured face of youth and candor with which I had so long been familiar. Jesuitical lines surrounded his mouth, and the eyes were brooding and perplexed. Very soon, at the announcement from the porter that "dinner was ready in the dining car," I followed Bryan and was placed by the porter at a table for two, in his company. With my knowledge of the pleasure all politicians have in the recognition of their personalities, I, without preamble, addressed him with the question, "Mr. Bryan, would you like to know what Bourke Cockran said to me about you the last time I saw him?"

"Why, yes, madame!" he replied, "I should be very glad to hear it."

"He said that you spoke better back to the galleries than any man he had ever seen on his feet."

This doubtless agreeable testimony from one orator to another was followed by much pleasant conversation, while I continued to ponder upon the writing I had seen upon my companion's physiognomy. Suddenly Mr. Bryan laid down his knife and fork and said, quite irrelevantly, "Do you believe, madame, that character finally writes itself upon the face?" At my surprised assent to the question which had been the subject of my own unspoken thoughts, "I have that conviction myself," he continued, "and believing this, you may imagine my feelings when an old friend said to me the other day, 'Bill, you used to have the face of an honest

140

man, but now it's the face of a demagogue and free silver is written all over it.' "

As an illustration of character-writing on human faces this was not only vastly amusing and confirmatory, but I also thought his relation of the scarcely flattering remark very sympathetically frank and even naïve. The papers I had seen him so gravely considering were shown to me and I found them to be notes of a speech for a Western college. These notes were a collection of singularly innocuous platitudes, which he believed were his own discoveries; the expression of a mind ill equipped for modern evolution, has again exemplified to the amusement of his country. The writing on his face, I concluded, expressed perplexity, but not deliberate intellectual dishonesty. His singular control of his party has, I believe, been due to his sympathetic knowledge of men, but the "spellbinder of the cross of gold" no longer charms his audiences and his party leadership has brought disaster.

CHAPTER ELEVEN

LONDON

THE success of "Robin Hood" changed our lives and finally cut all the ties which bound my husband so reluctantly to business and us to Chicago.

In this connection I may recall a conversation between my father and my husband's banker uncle, John de Koven. My father announced with satisfaction that in the brief period when my husband was in the credit department of the J. V. Farwell Co. he had invented a new system of credits which was a definite improvement. Mr. de Koven then observed, with the pardonable pride of his family, that the de Kovens all had ability. I then put in a word for my husband's musical talent, whereupon the successful banker and the successful politician both expressed the opinion that music should be considered as a diversion and should not be seriously followed. That there was reason enough for this opinion could hardly be denied, when my husband was, in fact, the only American who was seriously attempting a career in comic opera. It was hardly to be expected that he would be able to attain success or distinction in this new field and failing this, music as a profession was not a feasible or financially remunerative occupation. But just as we were on the wing for Europe, after "Robin Hood's" success, we found ourselves in New York at the same hotel, the old Brunswick, with

142

this skeptical uncle. A knock on the door was followed by Mr. de Koven's voice, declaring, as he handed me a morning paper, "Anna, I shall never speak to you again." The paper contained the statement that "Mr. John de Koven, uncle of the famous young composer, was stopping at the Brunswick." Another later instance of this vicarious reputation, so little appreciated by Mr. de Koven, was related by him with his characteristic humor. On a trip to the West, with a company of railroad magnates, headed by Mr. Villard, they arrived at Los Angeles, where at the station a crowd of several hundreds of enthusiastic admirers of "Robin Hood" was assembled to greet the composer, Mr. de Koven, whose presence had been announced on this railroad expedition. The disappointment of the Los Angeles assemblage, when it discovered that it was only the banker it was privileged to meet, was loudly expressed, to the amusement of Mr. de Koven's comrades of the railroads.

On our journey across the ocean we met the very opportunity which was destined to provide the larger audience and the increased reputation which my husband desired. On the steamer we became acquainted with a certain lovely Mrs. Sedgwick, accompanied by three even lovelier young daughters, one of whom, Anne Douglas, has become the celebrated writer of many novels. At the time she must have been about twelve years old, with the delicate features of her mother, large inquiring blue eyes, and waves of luxuriant hair which fell over her shoulders.

"What do you suppose it may mean?" her mother

143

asked me. "This child is already reading Keats and says, ' I don't understand it, mamma, but I should like to eat it?' "

We were surrounded during the voyage by the little lovely Anne and her pretty sisters, and when we landed met their father on the dock. Still very noticeable in his height and striking good looks, Mr. Sedgwick, who had formerly taken a very prominent part in the society of London, was at this time in touch with the theatrical world and it was he who took the score of "Don Quixote" to Horace Sedger, manager of the Prince of Wales' Theatre. This opera was immediately accepted and a contract signed for its London production. Here then was a very definite prospect. After a few weeks in London and a summer at Homburg, we installed ourselves in an apartment in Paris, where for a short period my husband had the great privilege of studying with Delibes. Our plans had most unfortunately to be altered, for Delibes suddenly died, and the very important opportunity of study with the French master, with whom my husband had already made very noticeable progress and composed several charming orchestral numbers, was ended. Very soon, also, there was another cause for our departure from Paris. The fame of the successful "Robin Hood" had reached England, and Sedger demanded that this opera should be substituted for "Don Quixote," and announced its immediate production in London.

Following the call of fortune, we gave up our Paris apartment and, crossing to London, there took a very pleasant house, No. 11 Egerton Gardens, and followed the rehearsals of the opera, which in London was called "Maid Marian." Fortune was not favorable as all our hopes and justifiable confidence had led us to believe. The "run" of "Maid Marian," although it never fell below the receipts demanded by the contract, was interrupted in the midst of its success by the production at the same theater, for afternoon performances, of a little musical pantomime called "L'Enfant Prodigue." This was a slight but very popular French novelty, with two Pierrots and one man at the piano, and it crowded the theater. Mr. Sedger saw double profit in displacing "Maid Marian," with its far larger cast and expenses, in favor of this pantomime, and put in on for the evening as well as the afternoon performances.

If this unexpected condition had not intervened to bring the London run of "Maid Marian" to an untimely end, it is highly probable that we would have remained in England, and as probable that the opera would have repeated its long career in America. The first performance was successful and the critical comments favorable, although Harry Smith's libretto suffered seriously from the unattractive clowning of the English singer, Monkhouse, whose drunken antics were sadly different from the high-comedy methods of Barnaby, an amusing drunkard, and never a brutal one, who was destined to please American audiences as the Sheriff of Nottingham for so many years. We were in a stage box on that memorable evening, with Mr. and Mrs. Waldorf Astor. King Edward, then Prince of Wales, was in the box below us, and the audience was full of well-known Americans in London. Oscar Wilde, then at the highest point of his renown, met us at the door, expectant of a congratulatory supper with Wyndham, an old and most loyal friend, and other actors. But Monkhouse had so troubled us with his forty minutes of clowning, and we so feared its result upon the audience, which, like all audiences, expect to be mildly and constantly pleased, but never forgive an interlude of boredom, that we had no heart for supper, and went back to our house with very mixed feelings.

The opera, however, settled down to a satisfactory "run," and fortune seemed favorable. A proposition to collaborate with Gilbert was one of its results for my husband, but all hope as far as England was concerned was blasted by the fate which awaited the opera, by the popularity, only for a few weeks, of "L'Enfant Prodigue."

We had many agreeable experiences in London, although the continued fog was very bad for my health, accustomed as I had always been to the clear and invigorating American climate. I wonder now, as I recall how warm a welcome was given us in London by the writers and actors, even before my husband's work was presented to a London audience, why we young and unknown Americans were so fortunate. At the house of Sir Edward Gosse we met at his Sunday afternoons many of the celebrated authors of the day—Andrew Lang, Thomas Hardy, Sir Walter Besant, and others. We dined at Mr. Rutledge's with Irving and Hare and Tree and others, a very gay dinner, as I remember. I met also, at Lady Seton's home in Chelsea, when she received all the literary people of the time, Oscar Wilde and George Moore. My first meeting with Oscar Wilde was at the rooms of Mrs. Montton, the American poetess, who annually took an apartment in London to receive her many London friends. "You must know Oscar Wilde," she said to me as I stood a few steps away from him. Quite definitely and with his characteristic posing he assumed a hesitating manner, and when finally led to my side, demanded in a loud voice which filled the little *salon,* "Where in the world do you come from?"

"You must guess," I naturally replied.

"From the South—oh yes, from the South—you are a creole!" This, as a tribute to my dark eyes and hair, was combined with the usual English interpretation of the significance of the word "creole," and was hardly sympathetic to me.

"I was born in Chicago," I was moved to reply.

There was horror in his expression as he answered, "Never, no, never; your parents have deceived you." But we met later and often and he used sometimes to visit our house, walking with me in the little garden and talking as only Wilde could.

At one luncheon at my house the conversation of the company, which included not only Wilde, but Henry James, George Moore, John Hay, and Mr. Smalley, was very brilliant, and a great compliment, as I considered it, to the young hostess. Mr. James, in commenting upon Wilde's extraordinary eloquence, said that it did not exceed that of others in its richness of metaphor, but was absolutely unique in its wit. Wilde on this occasion ascribed his talents to his mother, of whom he spoke with the utmost affection and admiration. I contributed, as I remember, an example of my observation of the remarkable types of humanity to be seen in London. In the omnibus, in which on a late winter afternoon I was returning from a visit to Mrs. Archibald Forbes, who lived in Regent's Park, I had seen a man whose resemblance to the Greek Comic Mask had immediately arrested my attention. The eyes, scarcely visible, except for a sinister sunken glare out of deeply curved sockets, were precisely similar to those of the familar mask. The nose was also appropriately aquiline, and the mouth, leering and formidable, was set in the exact curve, with lips meeting in the center, which one sees in the mask. The low brim of a wide hat came over his brows, and a cloak was wrapped about the shoulders of this remarkable and mysteriously threatening individual. Beside him sat a frightened girl, whom he was regarding with a fixed and hypnotizing gaze. She was fair as a Greuze, with the aureole of blond hair and the smooth velvet cheeks of the French painter.

"Don't let that slip, Mrs. de Koven," exclaimed Wilde. "It is a most excellent theme for a story." For how many months I read Greek literature and studied Greek topography and history, to enable me to write the story entitled *The Comic Mask,* and afterward accepted by Macmillan's, I hardly like to remember! For the acceptance was conditional on my supplying other stories of a like character, to make a book. In my search for similar topics I traveled far, and finally discovered a theme in Herodotus, and his story of the sister of that Artaxerxes who was the Ahasueras of the

148

Old Testament, and who, according to the historian, was the "most beautiful and the most intemperate woman in all Asia." But in developing the story, I found and wrote a book much too long to be a companion to *The Comic Mask,* and when published, under the title of *By the Waters of Babylon,* it was considered to be more suitable for a play than a novel. Turned duly into a melodrama, it was actually accepted by Belasco, and at this promising juncture the long series of developments which followed Oscar Wilde's advice were most unluckily arrested by the theatrical war raging in the year 1895 between Belasco and the firm of Klaw & Erlanger. The latter company was at the time producing four of my husband's operas, and served notice that all his operas would be withdrawn from the stage if a play by his wife was produced by Belasco. The play was actually accepted and the cast in process of assembling, but there was no alternative, as all our income came from my husband's operas, and with great difficulty Belasco was induced to return it to me.

Those of the present generation who remember the card scene in the "Girl of the Golden West" will recall that it was the best scene in the play. It was the best scene in *my* play, and the idea of the two opponents playing for the life of a man was my idea and gathered from the accounts in Herodotus of dice-playing in Babylon. Klaw & Erlanger promised to produce the play, but never fulfilled this promise and so perhaps the best work of my best days is unpublished and unperformed.

London was very interesting during the winter of

149

1890. The Ibsen plays were given at matinées, when the audiences contained many of the literary and theatrical figures of the day. Pinero's "Mrs. Tanqueray" made then its remarkable success, and Henry Arthur Jones, whom we knew, was also producing his best plays.

I wrote dramatic criticisms in those days for a Chicago paper, and was treated with far more respect than I expected or deserved by the playwrights. We knew a few people, whose numbers were gradually increasing, in the other world of London. We met them at Mr. and Mrs. White's, who were cousins of my husband. We stopped with Mr. and Mrs. Chamberlain, whom I had known in Washington. At Highbury I listened to Lady Dorothy Neville's witticisms and witnessed her amusement over a hot combat between Mrs. Chamberlain and her eldest stepdaughter, the subject being the moot question of the American use of some unimportant words, such as window shades, which we use instead of the English *blinds*. And I wondered over such persistent argument for the correctness of the American use of the word for the object which shuts out the sunlight. I avoid the word, for I am by no means as certain as Mrs. C. was of the reasons for her argument, but, as I remember, this was an attitude which she had evidently found imperative, even in the most minute cases.

I was presented at court on account of my father's political position in the diplomatic circle, and, curiously enough, was the very first person to make my curtsy to Queen Victoria on that occasion. Introduced by Lady

MRS. REGINALD DE KOVEN
LONDON, 1891

MRS. CHATFIELD TAYLOR
LONDON, 1891

Salisbury, the Queen asked to have my name repeated, being, apparently, quite interested in this one of the many Drawing Rooms of her long reign and intending to be amused at the spectacle. So were also all the row of other royalties headed by the Princess of Wales, exquisite as always in a beautiful red dress, and the other princesses, when I passed successfully in a series of sweeping curtsies. I was also invited to a court ball and there saw several of the great ladies who made Queen Victoria's court so famous. Lady Warwick, then Lady Brooke, was young and faultlessly lovely, dressed in blue and white, with many diamonds, a reincarnation, I thought, of one of those Roman empresses we read of in the pages of history, in her complete classic type and also in the flutelike sweetness of the voice I had heard of, and in her erratic and ungovernable temper. Like Ethelfreda or Boadicea was Lady Londonderry in her diamond crown. As classic as Lady Warwick, but of a fuller, more triumphant beauty, the Duchess of Leinster united the sadness of a "Princesse Lointaine" with the culminating perfection of humanity's idea of divinity, looking, indeed, not so much like a goddess as like Apollo himself. Beside her was the Duchess of Portland, in black with a bunch of her famous carnations, and Mary Leiter on Rosebury's arm.

It was to me a thrilling spectacle of England's best. Here assembled in court dress were its peers, Anglo-Saxon, but in their clear-cut features similar to that procession of Senators on the famous bas-relief in the Roman Forum. Here were the women, classic also in their physical type, and all representing the evolution

151

of a great people and its attainment to actual perfection in both distinction and beauty. The great red-and-gold drawing-room at Buckingham Palace, with its gold plate piled to the ceiling, was never more brilliantly magnificent than in this season of 1890, when fashion still commanded the display of famous inherited jewels on each lovely head and when ball dresses were splendid with their sweeping brocades. I went also to several other balls of the season—to Mrs. Mackay's at Carleton House Terrace and to Mrs. Roberts's. Robert Lincoln was our ambassador, and I was very often at the Embassy. My husband's aunt, Mrs. Robert LeRoy, came to stop with us in the spring of that year, 1890, and was, in spite of her years (she had been a famous beauty in Paris during the reign of Napoleon III) a highly amusing guest. With her I went to the French Embassy presided over by her old friends Mr. and Mrs. Waddington. We went also to the Foreign Office, where Mrs. Ronalds, with her characteristic amiability, took me by the hand and, going through the rooms, introduced her young compatriot to everyone she met. Commenting on her remarkable history, the Russian ambassador, with whom I was talking at the French Embassy, as Mrs. Ronalds approached us exclaimed, *"Quelquefois, madame, c'est la vie, et quelquefois c'est la mort."* It was *la vie* for this victorious *charmeuse,* who could survive any defiance of conventions, could preside at the head of the harem of the Khedive of Egypt, could wander with various companions all the world over, and yet by the witchery of her unforgotten smile, her enchanting voice, her unfailing courage, and above all by her wonderful amiability, which never failed of an opportunity to make friends, by numberless little obliging acts, such as I had experienced, could triumphantly make her place in London, and hold it unquestioned to the end of her long life. I went, of course, very often to her musical afternoons, when singers and pianists and composers offered willingly their talents for her own pleasure and that of her many friends.

My sister, Mrs. Chatfield Taylor, went with me to several balls, and as she walked through the rooms, that London society which, as Henry James said, always gives instant tribute to beauty, murmured in admiration at the vision of youth and loveliness which so briefly appeared in their midst. She was tall, and often garbed like a flower, in rose satin, which matched the fresh rose of her exquisite, smiling face. The description of my humble situation between my beauty and my genius was just enough, as I somewhat ruefully noticed in a newspaper comment upon the "beautiful Mrs. Chatfield Taylor, sister of the wife of the celebrated young composer."

Young enough my husband was, in fact, and he looked much younger than he was, at that time, which was proved when he first went to the Prince of Wales' Theatre to see the manager. Left for an unaccountably long time in the outer office, a secretary finally approached him and asked when his father could be expected. When my husband replied that his father was no longer living, the astonished exclamation, "It is not possible that you are the Mr. de Koven we have been waiting for!" greatly amused him.

We had need to be young and optimistic, for the close of the opera cut off royalties, and we returned to America in the summer of 1890.

I wonder, as I recall our entirely care-free mood as we left our London house, with the consciousness that fate had decreed so undeserved a limitation of my husband's musical hopes and ambitions, why that mood was so happy. We had burned our boats, abandoned Chicago and its business opportunities, and had neither home nor definite occupation to which to return, and also very little money in our pockets. But fortune, which had only turned away for a moment, was awaiting us on the shores of our own country. On landing in New York, we went first to Narragansett Pier, and then to visit Mr. Van Alen at Newport, whose acquaintance we had made in London at the house of his old friend, Lady Seton.

According to the custom of Newport hosts and hostesses, no invitations were asked for their guests. But my husband had many old Newport friends whom he had known as a boy, during a brief residence of his family in America's summer capital, and we continued to enjoy our youth and our opportunities, with the same disregard for the future as had supported us when we left England. "Robin Hood," although successful in the first two weeks trial in Chicago, and successful in a season at the Tremont Theater in Boston, had not yet been given in New York. So at this critical moment of our history, and during the summer of no performances, we were in receipt of no income from the opera. But, according to my husband's contract with the company, a season in New York was obligatory. The Bostonians had never been a metropolitan company, preferring the less exacting audiences of what in theatrical parlance were called the "provinces." But in pursuance of the contract, they had leased for a few weeks in September an abandoned theater called The Standard, which had been, for its persistent bad fortune, dubbed the "Morgue." Here "Robin Hood" began its New York existence. For two weeks the theater was empty. No "star" known to New York shone in that company, whose excellence was due primarily to the equal ability and good acting of its male members. But at the beginning of the third week of the announced month of its run, suddenly the theater was crowded to its doors. Well I remember my sensations as I sat with my husband in the theater on the Tuesday night of the last week, in seats which we with difficulty obtained. It had arrived, our ship of good luck—a good ship indeed, whose argosies of fame and fortune were destined to supply all needful income for twenty years and to make my husband's name a household word in our country. Another surprise awaited my husband when in the window of his publisher's shop he saw piled up copies of "Oh, Promise Me" and others of his songs. "What do you suppose it can mean?" he asked me, with the simple modesty at his own success which always characterized him.

Another piece of good luck arrived at that time in a curious fashion. At the close of our visit in Newport I returned to my father's house in Lake Forest, leaving my husband still at Mr. Van Alen's. He had been asked to stop over a week-end with Mrs. George Scott, but, manlike, he had mistaken the date of the invitation and arrived at Mrs. Scott's house on the wrong Saturday. Urged to remain under its ample roof, he there met Mr. Ballard Smith, then managing editor of the New York *World,* and he, quickly recognizing the promise and ability of my husband, and seeing the brilliancy of the rising star of comic opera, then and there offered him the position of musical critic on the *World.* Thus in a few weeks our plans were decided, and in October, 1890, we came to New York to live.

CHAPTER TWELVE

THE house we took in New York, at 4 West 39th Street, belonged to Mrs. Charles Sackett. "What," said all my new acquaintances, "have you got Mary Alice's house?" The popularity and well-known habitat of this old New Yorker no doubt assisted these new acquaintances in locating our residence. It was all very new and exciting to us during that first winter, and I doubt if we realized how easily the new broom swept the cobwebs from our sky. We went almost every night to the opera, sometimes in the boxes and sometimes in the seats alloted to the critic of the New York *World*. Mrs. Kernochan, who was noted for her extraordinary observation and no less extraordinary memory, gave me a charming example of this observation one evening at the opera. I was sitting alone and quite lonely in my downstairs seat, while my husband was away in the critic's room, when Mr. Kernochan suddenly appeared beside me, saying, "Kitty thinks you might like to come to our box; you seem a little lonely, my dear."

Dear Mrs. Wilson often invited me to her box, and once as I was leaving my seat at the close of the opera she bent and kissed my shoulders, saying, "Forgive me, my dear; I couldn't help it." All her three daughters inherited her sweetness and ability, her knowledge of the world, and her appreciation of its prizes. My husband's early friendship for all the family, begun long ago in Newport, brought us much and continual pleasure in our New York life.

Mrs. Whitney, whom I knew in Washington when her husband was Secretary of the Navy, was also exceedingly kind to us, both in New York and in Newport. She asked us to come to her luncheon table as often as it was possible, and I like to remember the smile on the face of the servant who opened the door to me the last time I availed myself of this invitation. Mrs. Whitney's incurable malady had reappeared and I realized that she was doomed when I was shown to her boudoir to take my luncheon with her. That she also knew her fate was only too clear as she gazed, like Mr. Blaine, on her death-stricken hand. She reviewed her past life, telling of her blessings and speaking of her brother, who, unknown to her had one day pinned a check for two million dollars on her pincushion. "Was there ever such a brother?" she asked me. Sweetness and generosity were synonyms for the character of this dear woman.

Mrs. Paran Stevens was at this time the hostess of probably the only approach to a *salon* (a very abused word) which New York ever possessed. First at her house in a lower side street, and afterward in the spacious rooms in the house (now a bank) at the corner of 57th Street and Fifth Avenue, I was a frequent guest. This remarkable woman, who, as every one knows, began as a factory girl in Lowell, was as witty as she was kind, and of equal courage and high spirit. She was already an old woman when I knew her first, bearing all the scars

of her battle with life. Sometimes she was far too out-
spoken, for her temper became increasingly difficult, but
she had inexhaustible vitality and a remarkable social
flair, which could distinguish before anyone else the
first gleam of any rising star. How many brilliant
careers have been launched under her eyes—how many
marriages arranged—only she knew, but that she often
experienced ingratitude from the stars when finally
swimming high in the firmament she once admitted to
me. "Those I——s I have booted and stockinged them.
I have introduced them to everyone they know, and now
they do not even call on me when I go to London."
And of her daughter, Lady Paget, I once heard her
say, "There's a lady, my dear; you would never believe
she was *my* daughter." Yet when I asked her questions
of her far-away youth, she replied, "Oh yes, my dear,
I had everything, yes, everything." Everything meant
youth and intelligence and beauty, I supposed, all but
good birth and training, but without this, there was
never an American woman who made such use of every
gift and opportunity. During those last years, when
she was keeping up her *salon,* she used to take a cab—
for then there were no telephones—and scour the city
for friends and strangers to fill her rooms. When she
died, alone except for the presence of an old New
Yorker, Mr. Otis, who told me he did not think it right
that she should be quite abandoned in her last hours,
she left her place quite empty. New York has never
had a second Mrs. Stevens.

There were several series of balls during that winter
and for a number of years following—one at Delmon-

ico's, the old and famous Delmonico's, at the corner of
Madison Square—conducted by Ward McAllister, the
solemnly devoted social arbiter, who firmly believed that
his mission was to allot the proper places to every one in
the social heaven. "Is this true?" he exclaimed as he
met me one day in the company of Mrs. Robert LeRoy,
who mentioned our relationship. "If I had known it,
I would have assigned you a very different place. Why
did you not tell me you are her niece?" The Four
Hundred, whose limited scope really did include what
was best in New York in those days, was his enumera-
tion if not his creation. If one was accorded a place
among these elect, no ball was given without an invitation to each member of the Four Hundred. There was,
therefore, a far greater solidarity among all these people
fortunate enough to be included, and social influence
and social talents were far more appreciated and far
more powerful than in the years which have followed,
when the unwieldy size of the city has broken that solidarity and made all assemblages a choice, and a very
arbitrary one sometimes, between the *dejecta membra*
of this once very *fermé* society.

We began even in that first winter to receive musi-
cians, and my first acquaintance with Paderewski was
when he dined with us in our little house in 39th Street.
Did he talk music, this prince of the piano? Not at all.
His discourse, which might have done honor to any
Englishman, was about pre-Shakespearian dramatists.
That first winter of 1891-92 he made the conquest of
New York. Looking like an archangel of the "Omar
Khayyám" illustrations, with a Polish fire and pride

160

and his flashing wit and good fellowship, he was as gay as any schoolboy. How well I remember the two concerts he gave in Chase's studio, and the enthralled audience in those tapestried rooms! How amused I was at his reply to a scarlet-clad lady, scarlet even to slippers and gloves, when she announced that she had nearly fallen on the slippery stairs, nearly lost her life in her effort to reach him! He was standing at bay, behind a large punch bowl, and his instant reply, at which she turned in a whirl of red skirts and keen although laughing embarrassment, was, *"Alors, madame, l'enfer a perdu quelquechose."* How often, in the many conversations I have been privileged to enjoy with this noble friend, have I been interrupted in some banality by flashes of wit quite as disconcerting as, but far more amiable than, the reply I have quoted. As an interpreter of character, this arch-interpreter of music was and is unique. Out of a cloud of clairvoyant perception, his words, deeply comprehending of the best of one's inner motives, have often brought me unforgettable assistance. As a friend he is unrivaled, as my husband, whom he deeply loved, most gratefully realized.

The little house on 39th Street, furnished with almost Lilliputian chairs and sofas, which my tall friends of the Stock Exchange and of the Knickerbocker Club, and the musicians, found very uncomfortable, was only inhabited by us for one winter. But although so small and so temporary a residence, it was a very busy abode. The "Fencing Master," my husband's next operatic success, was written there and, with Marie Tempest in the title rôle, was a definite addition to both fame and income. The "Knickerbockers," somehow composed in the interval between London and New York, although considered by the Schirmers quite equal to "Robin Hood," was one of those unaccountable failures which seem inevitably to occur in all composers' careers. But the public was so engrossed with its first love, "Robin Hood," that all succeeding works actually suffered in comparison, as if its admirers were jealous of any rivals. Almost my husband was induced, as was amusingly told in one of Frank Stockton's best stories, to take, like the perplexed hero of the tale, another name, which should not be obscured by the unequaled success of a first popular work. "You will never down 'Robin Hood,' my boy," Joseph Jefferson said one day to my husband. "I have had to play 'Rip' all my life; the public would not have me in any other rôle."

My husband's position as critic of the New York *World* took us constantly to concerts and the opera, and brought him into close association with his *confrères* of the other journals. Among these was James Huneker, still young enough, ruefully, to regret his disappointed ambitions to become a pianist and very enthusiastically criticizing musicians. The remark he made about De Pachmann I do not think has been published. This incomparable interpreter of Chopin had the fantastic manners of a monkey at the piano, indulging in the most remarkable gestures and audible grunts of dissatisfaction if his fingers became rebellious, and Huneker called him "The Chopanzee." During the years when he was critic my husband much enjoyed his companionship with his friends in the critics' room at

162

the Metropolitan Opera House, and there one evening
he noticed that Mr. Huneker's cuffs were plentifully
sprinkled with ink.

"Jim, it seems to me that you are like Mr. Boffin," he
said.

"I don't see why," replied Huneker. "I haven't a
bower. Oh yes, I have—left bower, all right."

The left-handed domestic arrangement of which he
was the temporary hero was the reason of this correc-
tion.

It was my good fortune to receive much encouragement in my humble literary ambitions from Mr. Huneker, and although temperamentally both choleric and
erratic, he was, I think, very fond of my husband. Mr.
Krehbiel's critical ability consisted of his vast knowledge
of musical literature. His judgment of anything
modern was distinctly unreliable. Of "Robin Hood,"
on its first New York production, he said "that, like a
first litter of puppies, it deserved drowning, although
the puppies showed promise." In later references he
called it the "classic of American comic opera."

After that first New York winter we spent the summer of 1892 in Newport, in a little rented house, and
enjoyed the bathing, the coaching parties which were
then very popular, and numerous balls. I found, however, that my topics of conversation were not greatly
appreciated by the *jeunesse dorée* of that period. I was
not willing, and perhaps not able, to forget my wider
and more varied associations with the politicians and
writers whom I had known in Washington and London,
so with a new and delightful friend, Stewart Merrill,

163

an American-born poet of the then rising symbolic school in France, I walked and sailed, talking happily of his literary work and ambitions, and sometimes watching his amused expression as he looked at the whirling dancers at the Casino. His habitat had been the Quartier Latin, and he preferred it to Newport.

I was then a very frequent visitor at the house of Mrs. Daniel LeRoy, in this the last summer of her long life, and shall always treasure the memory of a very great lady, a lingering survivor of the days of my husband's grandfather, Jacob LeRoy, who was a cousin of her husband's. Witty and gracious, she was a model of the distinguished manners of that long past time, and often related anecdotes of my mother-in-law, whose wedding to the young clergyman she had attended.

The spectacle of the champion tennis matches occupied, as usual, a week of midsummer, and there was polo, golf also, which I then began to play, an innocent, if not particularly mind-filling, occupation. I was restless for my old friends, and with the impatience of youth longed for some more absorbing occupation than I realized that I should ever attain in the purely social activities of Newport.

Miss Adèle Grant, later Lady Essex, was at Newport that summer, and as finished in her graceful ways and exquisitely modulated voice as she was in the later days of her London residence. Lady Ribbesdale, then Mrs. Astor, and Miss Langdon, equally preserving the inheritance of beauty and race from their ancestors of the Colonial court of Philadelphia, were both in Newport that summer. The Belmonts and Havemeyers contributed to the not wholly uncalculating Anglo-American society a lavish generosity and hospitality, and a certain Austrian strain of reckless and self-forgetting emotion, not dissimilar from that of the Hapsburg grand dukes and princesses. Theodore Havemeyer, as I so often saw him as he drove his four-in-hand down the avenue, with a brilliant smile to all passing friends, was the model of gayety and prosperity and genuine joy of living, freely shared by all who knew him. James Parker, who was a very indulgent friend of my youth, will always be remembered for his whimsical face, with his white hair modishly cut over his dark eyes, another survivor of that old New York when it really was an aristocracy. "Every *chaçun* has his *chaçune*," he used to say somewhat ruefully, with a hint of his own remembrance of the time when a change of partners in life, which is now so easily and regrettably possible, was far more difficult to accomplish. His friend and contemporary, Peter Marie, Gallic in name as in his love of feminine beauty, dined at Mr. Parker's house while I was the only guest during a day's absence of my husband. Not to be outdone in gallantry, and jibing at each other for an "old fool," they alternately left the table to kneel at my feet, giving me an example of other times and other ways more fantastically expressive than ours, but surely more flattering than the present emancipated youth of our day has any opportunity of enjoying. Mrs. Stevens, who during many years kept a continually open house on Bellevue Avenue, never ceased her midnight talks with her always amused and loyal friends. "Midnight," she said, "is my 'magic hour.'"

A MUSICIAN AND HIS WIFE

Mrs. August Belmont, kindly visiting the stranger, which I was in those days in Newport, took me to drive in her little phaeton, in a charming hour which I have always remembered. The free privilege of recognizing charm and ability in new acquaintances surely should be the prerogative of assured position. The fear of compromising a lately secured position which makes for both cruelty and blindness, very definitely characterized our most representative society in this latter period. Not "small dance," alone, was written on invitation cards, but "very, very small," a description only too characteristic of an exaggerated exclusiveness.

Newport to the eyes of the observer, such as Stewart Merrill, was a fantastic and incomprehensible spectacle of useless activity. To me, whose vision was not so poetic a dream of the symbolistic expression of life, it was an epitome of America in a transition period, very luxurious in its ideas and expressions of enjoyment; very self-sufficient, and sometimes cruelly intolerant of the very existence of any who were not of their immediate order. The words, precisely similar to my own choice of expression regarding the deteriorating influence of the arbitrary supremacy of small coteries, which I heard from the lips of a great London hostess with an unequaled past of brilliant friendships and experience, testified to its existence in other countries and confirmed my opinion. Mrs. Paren Stevens, perhaps alone among those women who were not born to the purple, recognized that inclusiveness, intelligent inclusiveness, was far more interesting than exclusiveness, particularly

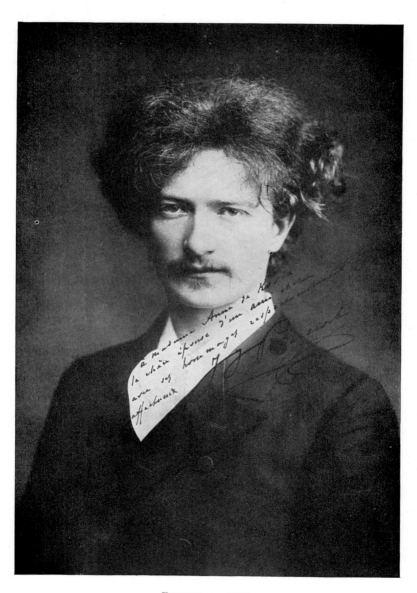

PADEREWSKI, 1892

when that exclusiveness was purely arbitrary and based on no brilliant endowment of mind or personality.

The exclusiveness of the eighteenth century in France was based on a different choice and different standards. The long deliberations of Madame du Deffand and her circle of wits before a candidate for her suppers was deemed worthy of admission, on the ground of his proved capacity to contribute either wit or wisdom to her circle of immortals, might well be imitated. A chop for a chop is too often the rule for invitations in all Anglo-Saxon countries, whether on this or the other side of the Atlantic.

With these and similar reflections, born of my early and determining experiences in diplomatic and political Washington and in literary London, I prepared for my second winter in New York.

CHAPTER THIRTEEN

WE took the unexpired lease of the house at 83 Irving Place from Mrs. Burton Harrison, and until its expiration, when we were able to introduce our own furniture, lived among the Colonial mahogany of this well-known Southern lady and writer. The opportunities, at first unrealized by either my husband or myself, of uniting under this roof the leaders of the musical and the worldly world of New York were very soon presented to us. The hint that this was our opportunity came from a woman whose life history has been so tragically inexpressive of what I now realize was a very unusual intelligence, that I now, over thirty years later, render her this tribute. I rejected her suggestion with, I fear, very scant recognition of its kindly and impersonal well-wishing, but the hint thus whispered soon became a decree, announced in the following circumstance. A consultation between my husband and myself as to how best we might return the hospitalities so generously offered to us, during our first winter in New York, led to the decision to give, as seemed to us appropriate, a musical party. Following this decision, my husband went to a musical bureau and asked to engage Woolf and Hollman, the well-known violinist and 'cellist of London, then for the first time in New York. On receiving the unexpected reply that these artists

168

would probably have great pleasure in playing for him, but that, as he was a professional musician himself, they would not be willing to accept any payment, my husband asked me if I thought he was a "professional musician" and whether I thought we could accept such a favor from strangers. I agreed with him that he was not a "professional musician" and also with his decision to pay these distinguished artists. Not yet, even in spite of his successful operas, had we forgotten his non-professional antecedents. But a second visit to the bureau disclosed the fact that Woolf and Hollman, having been apprised of our desire for their appearance at our house, had indeed expressed their willingness to come to us, and an equally fixed determination never to accept any payment from a musical *confrère*. And so we gave our first *musicale* in the Irving Place house, the first of very many, which, with intervals of absence and illness, have been continued from that year of 1892 until 1925.

Sometimes, as at this first party, we received the musicians, and the friends asked to hear them, in the evening. Afterward, on Sunday afternoons. The example, so generously followed, of Woolf and Hollman, of giving us and our friends their lovely art for nothing, became general with the fully launched singers and instrumentalists of that day, after Paderewski lent his own incomparable name to this custom and example. It is perhaps quite singular that my husband's success, and this, its most delightful sequence, should have come so early in our lives. Just out of our twenties, with unimpaired youth and enthusiasm, our experiences with the singers and artists of the piano, violin, and 'cello were a continual joy and even excitement.

No one of the company which was assembled in our house in the winter evening when Paderewski played will, I think, ever forget it. It was indeed a day such as only the fellowship of such gifted beings can make unforgettable. First my husband and his old friend, the violinist Adamowski, himself a very early friend of Paderewski, lunched with the master and other musicians, returning just in time for the dinner which preceded the *musicale*. The program was to consist of violin-playing by Adamowski, the piano, by Nikisch, and singing by his wife. Paderewski was at first only a listener. "Is Paderewski going to play?" asked one of my guests. "For if he is not, I am going home." "I cannot ask him," I replied, very naturally astonished at this demand, when a stir and a murmur came from his vicinity, and suddenly, with a dramatic toss of his head with its bright aureole of hair, he advanced to the piano. Not often has this great master given this pleasure to his friends, although he is far from niggardly when his friendly enthusiasm moves him to accord it, but never was generosity more warmly appreciated. After the audience of invited guests had departed, including the lady who had so boldly demanded to hear Paderewski, the musicians stayed on to a supper, or breakfast, which, at five o'clock, finished the day and the night and the morning passed in the master's company.

All that winter and during the many which followed while we lived in Irving Place, these musical parties were repeated. Abbey and Grau, then managers of

the Metropolitan Opera House, were very loyal friends
of my husband's, and made no objection to the concur-
rence of the Metropolitan singers in these afternoons
and evenings. Melba and Calvé and Schumann-Heink,
Plançon and Maurel and La Salle and the two de
Rezkés and Sembrich all sang for us very frequently,
and soon it became the ambition of the débutant musicians to ask to appear in this company. Thus soon I
found myself, for my husband left its conduct almost
solely to me, the manager of an unpaid musical bureau.
I was busy at my desk until midafternoon, and felt it
very little effort thus to make our contribution to New
York, whose leaders and lovely young representatives
(we were all young in those days) so willingly availed
themselves of our invitations. But how can I thank the
musicians for their generosity and good fellowship, and
how ever forget the many hours of pure delight which
the unusual combination of so many stars singing together in our firmament contributed to our joy of life
when life was in its heyday?

Very often, naturally, these musician friends of ours
dined with us in intimate and unforgettable *comité*.
The two de Rezkés and Paderewski, in sallies of irre-
sponsible gayety and anecdote, were unequaled dinner
guests. When Jean and Edouard first came to fill my
drawing-room with their twin magnificence of height
and beauty, for they were truly magnificent to look at
in those days, they did not greet me, but, looking at each
other, they asked, "Who does she resemble?" The name
of a certain Russian lady, since then departed in the
midst of her country's ruin, sprang to their lips, and

171

then Edouard exclaimed, with his unequaled bonhomie and audacity, *"Regardez la moi—est que ce n'est pas un petit coquin du printemps?"* Hardly *printemps* for me, but, after all, not very far from that period. The gay little compliment to my youth and freshness has often occurred to me, when I think of the great singer, the loving and enthusiastic friend, and the incomparable wit dying alone in a Polish cellar during the war. One conversation I had with Jean de Rezké is worth repeating. I told him that I perceived in the expression of his eyes a certain cool detached criticism which seemed to me very significant. "You are right," he replied. "I never forget at any moment of excitement my reason or my criticism of my own actions. This has guided me during all my life." Again discussing the long scene at the end of "Tristan and Isolde" he replied to my question as to whether he himself felt all Tristan's grief, that "his garments and even the couch on which he lay were wet with his tears." So much for the old problem of whether a singer or an actor should feel the emotions of his rôle. One of the most interesting of the incidents which added so much charm and excitement to our lives was the appearance of Madame Calvé in our drawing-room, when not only did she sing the music of "Carmen," but danced with unforgettable grace the *habanero*. Plançon, who was one of our most amiable friends, sang for us very frequently, with that marvelous voice, half velvet, half thunder. On one occasion, however, he greeted my husband with unusual reserve. *"Il faut que vous avez quelquechose contre moi, mon cher de Koven,"* he was finally persuaded to explain, *"vous avez dit que*

172

moi, moi—Plançon—était acceptable!" The trouble was that in one of his many criticisms of "Romeo and Juliet" my husband had thus too briefly referred to him in the rôle of Friar Laurent.

On another long-remembered occasion Plunkett Green and Marie Brema sang Goring Thomas's "Time's Garden" at our house. Tears were the expression of the emotion of my guests at this deeply moving duet sung by those beautiful young people, lovers then, as we were told, who poured out their hearts to us on that long-ago winter evening. Marie Tempest in the winter of 1893-94, who was then singing in my husband's opera, "The Fencing Master," also sang for us, to the great delight of my husband's friends of the Knickerbocker Club.

Near by, at the corner of Irving Place and 17th Street, was the house where Miss Marbury and Miss De Wolfe also were at home on Sunday afternoons. There I often went, when the winter months were over and I was free to enjoy their rival "days" and join in the always amusing conversation of the writers and artists whom they gathered about them. In a book very charmingly written by Eliot Gregory, about New York and its society, he says that among all the houses of hospitality in the great city, that of Miss Marbury and Miss De Wolfe and our own were the only ones where society and distinguished artists met together.

For many years it was our habit to group our friends of New York around some interesting stranger such as Madame Réjane, and Coquelin, Saint-Gaudens, or Ysaye, and always, and as often as he came to New York —Paderewski. And sometimes, after our musical parties, we were quite youthfully gay and played games with our guests, as when Sir Herbert and Lady Tree joined in the game of "catch the feather," seated on the floor under a blanket, with an uproarious circle, Sir Herbert solemnly blowing out his cheeks to drive the feather away from his neighborhood.

In one of my conversations with Tree I discussed the international subject of American and European women and declared that, although my sisters of America might bend, they never fell, for their feet were planted on Plymouth Rock. "Ah," said Tree, with his eyes turned to the ceiling, "it is so different in England; there the heart of the Englishwoman opens to sentiment as midnight flowers to the rays of the moon." A remark which hardly illustrated the humor for which he was so justly celebrated.

My sister, Mrs. Chatfield Taylor, was with me during the month of Tree's stay in New York, and together we enjoyed the many amusements of the city, assembling our respective friends and, as ever, redoubling our joys, of which none was keener than just being together. The horse show at Madison Square Garden, then a very gay spectacle, the theater, the opera, the balls, we attended, my sister as ever drawing all eyes to her beauty and enchaining all hearts by her gayety and always intelligent interest in all her new acquaintances. The controlling interest of our lives was the successful production of my husband's operas. After the "Fencing Master" with Marie Tempest, whom my husband always found most artistically intelligent, even if intractable at times, he wrote "Rob Roy," which has been considered by some critics to be superior to "Robin Hood." The "Mandarin," although very melodic and charming, was overshadowed by the "Geisha" of similar subject, and did not long hold the stage. The "Algerian," which contained some delightful music, was, like many modern comic operas, hampered by an incompletely successful "book," and failed, as was inevitable, to satisfy audiences, which too well remembered the Gilbert librettos. And also, at this time, Miss Tempest, caught in one of her sentimental episodes, left suddenly the cast of the opera, of which she was the principal, to join the hero of this episode in the opera in which he was performing. The "Algerian" was produced in Boston without any star of visible brilliancy, and conducted by my husband himself in a vain effort to save it from utter failure. On the opening night we witnessed the sad and silent departure of the entire audience after the second act in a crash of ill fortune which might well have discouraged any composer. My husband's eyes were afflicted also, at this critical juncture, by a severe attack of conjunctivitis, but on our return to the hotel, he exclaimed, with the courage which never abandoned him, "Never mind, when my eyes get better, I will write another opera."

"Other operas" followed immediately, as a result of his incessant industry and his really heroic devotion to his life's ambition. Two for Anna Held, "Papa's Wife" and "The Little Duchess," were gay vehicles for her beauty and vivacity, and very successful financially, although by no means as ambitious musically as my husband was capable of producing. But "Robin Hood," "The Fencing Master," and "Rob Roy" still held the stage, the latter two for four years, and "Robin Hood," as it seemed, perennially. During these years from 1892 to 1897 my husband was critic of the *World*, and with never ceasing composing, long and trying rehearsals, and our habit of dining out almost continually, his energy and health and really astonishing productivity were put to severe tests. The social life of that time was organized and imperative, and in addition to the entertaining which fell to our lot of the distinguished artists and writers and musicians, we had our part in the intimate alliance of the very agreeable people who lived near Gramercy Park. Mrs. Stuyvesant Fish lived just opposite me on Irving Place, and my intimacy with her, the most brilliantly witty as well as the most original and generous hostess of New York for many years, began at this time. Mr. and Mrs. Abram Hewitt, in the lovely treasure-filled house which was for so long the chief and most representative center of old New York, were on the opposite side of Gramercy Park, and Stanford White just opposite them on the west corner; Mr. and Mrs. Cooper Hewitt lived on the corner of Lexington Avenue near his parents, and Mr. and Mrs. Pinchot and Mr. and Mrs. Cowden faced the park on the north. Mr. White, although beautifying his house with a remarkable collection of objects brought from Europe, often gave parties in his rooms in the tower of the Madison Square Garden. To one of these we were invited. A crescent table was covered with old golden damask and spread with orchids, lights twinkled in surrounding bay trees, a mandolin band shed music like a sprinkling fountain, and about the table were women as lovely and varied in type as he ever assembled. Mrs. de Forest, with her Spanish eyes and irrepressible wit and grace, was there, and Mrs. Roche and her sister Mrs. Hewitt, beside Mrs. Ysnaga, a perfect blond beauty, in white and blue, with cheeks like wild roses, and Mrs. White, our hostess. Among the men, Bobby Hargous, Mrs. de Forest's brother, and the instigator of uproarous gayety always, Mr. Breese, Cooper Hewitt, and our host. And even before the end of dinner did we not all leave the table to dance about the room to the sound of the spraying music?

At another party, which soon followed this, I applauded one of these guests, with another gay beauty, as they danced on the dining table at five o'clock in the morning.

Just at this time, in the winter of 1895, Coquelin was in New York, and gave a supper for Jefferson, his devoted friend and *confrère,* devoted in spite of the fact that they could speak no word of each other's language. At this supper I sat next to Jefferson and listened to his anecdotes of the stage. "Do you remember seeing me in 'Camille'?" he exclaimed to the then Mayor of Brooklyn, Mr. Chapin. "I played Gaston. The supper was 'faked,' as we say; no such expense of staging in those days, and the 'super' who brought in the candles was drunk. As he set them down heavily on the table, one of the candles fell out and set fire to the ice cream; as the smoke curled up toward the ceiling, amid the titters of the audience, the actor who had left the stage was pushed back from the wings and, advancing to the table, solemnly blew out every one of the fourteen candles,

177

whereupon, amid roars from the laughing audience, the curtain was rung down! I think I am like Eugene Field," continued Jefferson, "who said he believed his French must be better than the English of his French friends, because they are so polite about it. Coquelin never laughs when I try to talk his language," he said, "but I always laugh at his English."

Henry Irving and Ellen Terry also gave suppers when they were in New York, as gay, with speeches and toasts, as the dinner which I shared with them in London, if not quite so intimate. On relating to Miss Terry that I had heard the account of the exhumation of Rossetti's book of sonnets to his dead wife from her coffin, by the very friend to whom this unpleasant duty was confided, Miss Terry said: "Oh yes, Rossetti was a great friend of mine. He was crazy, but I like 'em so! One day Rossetti asked us all to his house," she continued, "as he had a surprise for us. They were all assembled in the garden—his poets and his painters— when he suddenly opened a gate and let in a white bull, exclaiming, 'Janie Morris's eyes!' But the bull instantly charged upon the audience, who scattered with shrieks of terror." Mr. Watts Dunton told me in London of the life and loves of Rossetti, with whom he had lived for a number of years. The band of the pre-Raphaelites, while at Oxford in their student days, were so exalted by the discovery of the strangely beautiful woman whom they found in her father's tobacco shop in Oxford, that they decided that she must become the wife of one of the brotherhood, as she was the inspiration of each and every one of them. To Rossetti fell the choice, but already he had found the Beatrice of his wonderful picture, the inspiration of his poems, in the auburn-haired Elizabeth Siddall, whom he married. Thus the lot fell to William Morris. Mr. Dunton said that the deeply waved dark hair and the luxurious full lips of "Janie" Morris were due to a black strain in her blood. To my American prejudice against this strain its result in the case of this unique and haunting beauty, to make her the Egeria of the genius of England, at this period, seemed very strange and remarkable. Rossetti's love for this so idolized woman caused him to sadly neglect Elizabeth Siddall, who, languishing into consumption, departed from Oxford and went to the south of France. Remorseful at this tragic result of his infidelity, Rossetti summoned her back and married her, and when she died placed in her coffin the sonnets dedicated to her, declaring that they should never be published. But when Morris and Millais and Hunt achieved the fame which their poems and pictures deserved, his ambition also to take his place beside his brothers of the celebrated circle overcame his remorse, and hence the resolve to exhume the poems. One of Oscar Wilde's favorite themes during his visit to America, which he used to elaborate as he waved the so famous sunflower, was a thrilling evocation of the dark cemetery and the lantern-lit friends bending over the open coffin. This was true enough, but the detail so artistically added, that the golden hair of the dead woman had grown about the pages of the poems, was wholly imaginary, as the agent and executor of Rossetti's wishes affirmed to me, with a greenish tinge of remembered horror, as he related the story. I met him at a musical party at Holman Hunt's, the last surviving member of the pre-Raphaelite band. Around the walls hung the canvases of Hunt himself and of many others given him by the other painters of the school. A singer who, I was reverently informed, had been a pupil of Wagner, sang the Sword Song from "Siegfried," with quite appalling shrieks, which visibly stretched her long thin throat. Not a hint of anything but solemn delight could I see on the faces of the white-capped English matrons who listened, and when Madame Nordica, at the height of her fame, rose to follow the singer, in her red-velvet dress from Paris, she was very coldly received. English musical appreciation, as I have many times observed, is more sentimental than intelligent, as the loyalty to old favorites long past their prime has also so often expressed.

At my house in New York, and at Miss Marbury's, Max Beerbohm and all the delightful series of visitors from overseas, like Ellen Terry, brought similar stories of painters and poets and found most interested listeners. My own contribution to the knowledge of English poetry among my New York friends consisted in the establishment of what I called "The Browning Class." This idea, brought from Chicago, was very successfully realized. Sixteen of my friends consented together to assemble on each Monday morning at one another's houses, in turn, to listen to Mrs. LeMoyne as she read from the poet's works, and afterwards we discussed them at luncheon.

The contact with his vigorous drama with its optimis-

REGINALD DE KOVEN

tic messages was curiously stimulating to their minds, and the talks which followed very revealing of the characteristic opinions of the members of this class. After a while Mrs. LeMoyne read Ibsen also, and the ballads of Old England. One paraphrase of Swinburne on an old ballad form contained the couplet, delivered with dramatic intensity by Mrs. LeMoyne:

> "I put my maid in a dark shade
> I boiled my man in a brass pan."

A shriek from Mrs. Stuyvesant Fish, with the earnest declaration, "I should like to do it to mine," broke up that particular meeting of the class in uncontrollable merriment.

On another occasion the restlessness of human nature was declared by our teacher to be shared by the animal world, with the illustration of a story regarding a certain cow called Daisy, who was confined by its master to an island in a river. Mrs. LeMoyne, again more dramatic than humorous, announced, "But every few days Daisy *would* swim to the mainland." "Ah," said the deeply sympathetic voice of one of the class: "How well I understand! *I* am a Daisy."

How amusing, and I hope not wholly unprofitable, those classes were was proved by the fact that they continued for six years with unabated interest. Sometimes we ourselves read from the Browning plays—none of us, however, displaying great elocutionary talent, except Mrs. Fish, whose reading of the part of the Queen in the play "In a Balcony," for its unexpected dramatic comprehension and its clear and telling delivery, has always been remembered. Mrs. Astor, Mrs. Henry Sloane, Miss Hope Goddard, Miss Frelinghuysen, Mrs. Hewitt, Mrs. Baylies, Mrs. Clewes, Mrs. Roche, Mrs. Braze, Mrs. Goelet all met weekly for this poetic education. "What other new ideas," I was asked by a very attractive member of the other sex, "will you bring from Chicago? Why don't you organize a Kipling class?" Remembering my observation of more than one dedicated copy of Kipling's poems, in the houses of the lovely ladies upon whom he had bestowed them, I could only reply, "That is not necessary; you have one already."

CHAPTER FOURTEEN

THE summer months which intervened between the busy New York winters I usually spent in my father's house at Lake Forest. There also lived my sister Rose and her growing young family. And here I was reabsorbed in the life of parents and children, happy indeed with its open-air sports and the renewed home atmosphere. Golf had been lately initiated by Mr. Chatfield Taylor, first of its devotees in America, except for the company of Scotchmen who had founded a St. Andrew's Club near Yonkers. In the summer of 1892 tomato cans were sunk in our lawn and drinks were served for the golfers in our dining room. The links were small enough on the grounds of our place, and we often drove our balls over the near-by bluff of Lake Michigan. But our Lake Forest cousins and friends liked the new game so much that in the following summer a little farmhouse was leased by my brother-in-law and links laid over the prairie west of the railroad. Still later a large stone house was bought and the Onwentsia Golf Club was established. If my brother-in-law had foreseen the result upon real-estate values which his initiative in thus founding golf in Lake Forest was destined to produce, he might have greatly profited. The Chicago business men whose families had been compelled to spend their summers in Eastern

183

mountain and seaside "resorts" instantly took advantage of the new attraction at Lake Forest and, not only rented the cottages adjoining the golf club, but in increasing numbers bought land and built houses all over the unoccupied parts of the beautiful region. Two hundred acres of farm land in the prairie were bought by Mr. Ogden Armour, just west of the club, who called his property "Melody Farm" from the name of the original farmer who was thus in one night promoted to the rank of a capitalist. An Italian house with terraces like the Villa d'Este on Lake Como looked over Lake Michigan. This was built by Harold McCormick and rivaled in its magnificence the pink marble halls of Melody Farm. Polo soon followed at Onwentsia and national golf tournaments testified to the excellence of its links and brought throngs of Eastern golfers to Lake Forest.

"Golf, golf, golf!" my patient father only once exclaimed to his table of golf-mad children. "It is all you talk about."

How many golden summer afternoons we spent together, my sister Rose and I, on those sunset prairies, playing the entrancing game with two of our partners in conversational foursomes! With partners such as Bob and Evarts Wrenn the sport was quite excellent enough to satisfy our ambitions and to fill my mind with lovely memories. Over the wide surrounding fields, yellow as gold with mustard flowers, the sunset painted its glorious pageant of purple and gold, while my sister and I delighted, as always, in being together. Fairlawn was always overflowing with guests whom our parents per-

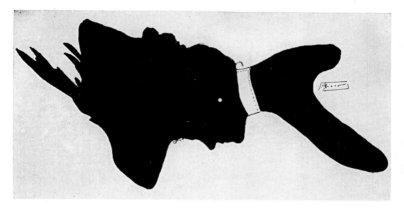

MRS. REGINALD DE KOVEN
NEW YORK, 1894

MR. DE KOVEN
NEW YORK, 1894

mitted us to invite as freely as if we were still unmarried children.

One return to the West was to visit my parents in their Chicago house by the Lake, for the World's Fair. The vision of the great architects which rose beside the sapphire lake remains in the memory of the multitude who saw it as an incomparable, though fleeting, projection of the American genius for architecture, which, in the Colonial variety and later in the amazing development of the skyscraper, has proved the greatness of the race. I saw the World's Fair first, very fortunately, in company with Stanford White, Charles McKim, and Frederick MacMonnies. The Fair was not yet opened to the public, and that great composition of buildings around the "Court of Honor" burst upon my eyes in purest beauty. In a little boat we rowed among the lagoons, while our guides pointed out to us the evanescent marvels thus magically summoned at the touch of their fancy. Later, when as the temporarily appointed Spanish consul, my brother-in-law escorted the Infanta Eulalia through the opened buildings of the great exposition, my sister and I were permitted to accompany him and the royal visitor. The Infanta was also accompanied by Admiral Davis, Mrs. Lodge's brother, representing the government, the Duca di Tamames, the Marchesa de Villa Hermosa, and others from the Spanish court. She was very gay and charming in those days, that somewhat fantastic Eulalia. A reception was given for her by Mrs. Palmer, then the head of the Women's Department of the exposition, and another at my father's house. My brother-in-law sometimes took us to the exposition on his coach, and on one of these parties Lady Curzon, then still Miss Leiter, Lady Ribbesdale, then Mrs. Astor, and my sister made a combination of famous beauties. At this time Paul Bourget, often a guest at my father's house, expressed his agreement with the opinions I have already quoted, saying that the society he found in Chicago was the best he had seen in our country. He also, with a rueful naïveté, remarked that "in France the old subjects are exhausted; there is only the old triangle of woman, husband, and lover to write about, only malicious and envious *confrères,* while in your great new country you have such magnificent subjects—the World's Fair, Niagara Falls, the *famille* Leiter!"

In the autumn of the year 1897, on returning to New York from my yearly summer visit to Lake Forest, I found my husband ill with typhoid fever. It was a long and serious illness and left him so weak and depleted of the vitality necessary for his double work as critic and composer, that I sublet the Irving Place house and we went to Washington for the winter. We were so happy in the far less strenuous life of the capital, so lured by the leisure of its wide streets and flowering parks, so warmly welcomed by my old Washington friends, that we remained there for five years.

The first house we leased was on 16th Street, and there on Sunday afternoons, and also on Wednesdays, I received the many new and old friends, who followed the Washington custom of calling on the several days of their friends, as well as on the stated days of the Senators' and Cabinet Ministers' wives.

186

My husband quickly recovered his strength in what was almost a holiday vacation for him, and enjoyed Washington quite as much as I, whose old associations, old as my childhood, made Washington in some ways far more like home than New York. Again I had the opportunity of receiving such musical friends as Paderewski, and at my table I have heard the talk of visitors from France such as de Regnier, and Coquelin, often accompanied by M. Jules Cambon, then French ambassador to our country, and his brilliant secretary, M. Thibault. Golf was very accessible at the Chevy Chase Club, and there on the sunny days which held far into February I would often drive in a little open victoria, with my bag of clubs and an agreeable conversational companion. McKinley was President, but, owing to Mrs. McKinley's delicate health, there was little entertaining at the White House. There was so much, however, in other houses, such as Mrs. Hitt's and Mrs. Hale's, and Mrs. Wetmore's, and Mrs. Hay's while John Hay was Secretary of State, that there was a continued series of dinners, each more amusing, according to my recollection of a very happy period, than the other. The collection of men to be chosen from in this city of politicians and diplomats was most interesting, and an opportunity for any hostess. At any one of the dinners I gave I could see about my table a Supreme Court judge, a Cabinet Minister, a leading Senator, and an ambassador, for of such was this society composed. We met continually at Mrs. McLean's house and at Mrs. Townsend's and there were several series of balls, and again, as in my girlhood, many excursions to Mt.

Vernon and the suburbs, and drives along the Potomac and its shaded shores, lined with flowering trees in the spring. Life was very easy, very informal, in the constant intimacy with daily encountered friends, in spite of occasional Diplomatic receptions at the White House, with their display of orders and decorations. Luncheons in the committee rooms of my senatorial friends were most amusing diversions, I hope, for the Senators, and certainly for me and the women who accompanied me. In pursuance of a certain measure in my father's interest, I met such a group one day in Aldrich's rooms as would have satisfied any ambition for interest and amusement. There was Aldrich himself, Hale and Wolcott, Wetmore and Alison, Mrs. Clarence Edwards and myself. Mrs. Edwards's wit called out such an ebullition of anecdotes and sallies of humor from Hale and Wolcott as I shall always remember. Wolcott, with a very melodious voice, great magnetism, and a facility of words which amounted to eloquence, was the most attractive man in the Senate, although not the most useful politically. His talk, as I have so often heard it at my own table and those of my friends, was like a fountain lightly spraying over every imaginable topic with fluid and brilliant comment. Albert Beveridge at this time had just arrived, like the young Lochinvar from Indiana, a really fresh breeze of intense personality, making demands for committee positions in the Senate upon his older and rather astonished *confrères*. He was filled with that *perfervidum ingenium* of his Scotch parentage, and growing in wisdom and becoming a finished scholar, as shown in his great biography

188

of Marshall, has more than fulfilled the promise of his
youth. His first appearance at my table, when he delivered an eloquent address to his hostess beside him,
has been followed by many games on the golf course
near Boston and many visits at his own beautiful house
at Beverly Farms. More than any one I have ever
known, he delights in the gifts and the good fortune of
his friends, a quality which endears him to all of them,
who themselves delight in the vigor, the wide knowledge, and the patriotism of this noble American, and
wish that his political activities might again, with his
added experience, be employed in our government.

I have spoken of my privilege of knowing M. Jules
Cambon. Upon him during the times that have tried
men's souls, both before the war and as ambassador to
Germany during the conflict and afterward, great and
serious responsibilities have fallen, and like Nestor
among the diplomatic powers, his advice and wisdom
have been critically important. I knew him before these
sadly serious days and delighted in his humor and always sympathetic comprehension of America and
Americans. He was very happy in Washington, I like
to remember, a warmly hospitable host, and a gay and
very affectionate companion, encouraging also, of all
the potential gifts of his young friends. He was, as I
remember, delighted to find in *Unleavened Bread,* the
novel by Grant, the Bostonian, a picture of an American woman which satisfied his French standards of de-
lineation of character. The heroine, studied from life,
was a rare type of American, for she was not only a very
successful *intrigante* but possessed of a "temperament,"

very rare among our countrywomen. I attempted to convince him that she was rare and not typical, and I hope his observations have confirmed my experience and my argument. He discussed the book with Roosevelt, in one of his many conversations with McKinley's successor. His own arguments were always pointed by a finger on his humorous nose, his face a picture of wise bonhomie and keen observation, delightful and friendly. He never dined alone while in Washington, when he was not himself the host at the French Embassy. Such an experience little prepared him for his next post at Madrid, as I was informed by one of his secretaries who ran breathlessly after me, one afternoon, in the Rue de la Paix. "The chief would never forgive me," he gasped, "if I did not speak to you; *figurez vous,* during the two years he has been at Madrid he has not dined out once." Such a record for the French ambassador casts a strange light on the society of the Spanish capital.

I saw Coquelin again in Washington during the winter of 1899, when he and Cambon used frequently to lunch and dine with me. On one occasion they supped with me in company with the minister of Belgium and his wife, and several others. The play, "Cyrano de Bergerac," in which Coquelin was then appearing in Washington, was the subject of our supper table discussion. The lady from Belgium, with some audacity, decried Rostand's poetry, and Coquelin, rising to his feet, declaimed several of the long soliloquies of Cyrano with a passion and rapidity never to be forgotten by the little company. He declared that he adored the play and his

Left to right: Mrs. Richard McCreery, Mrs. Tooker, Mr. McCreery, Miss Cameron, Miss Tilly Allien, Mr. Nonez, Mr. R. de Koven, Miss Eleanor Robinson, Miss Irvine, Miss Edith Grant, Mrs. de Koven, Mr. Clarence Wadsworth, Mr. Lorillard Kipp

rôle, which had finally given him an opportunity to conceal the ugliness and mediocrity of appearance which he confessed had been a life-long affliction. His bourgeois nose, he declared, had been submerged by the proboscis of Cyrano and he was free to be as romantic as he had always longed to be. "Ah, madame," he said as he resumed his seat, *"ma mère ne m'a pas fait beau."*

It was Cambon's pleasure to bring to my table the several French visitors who came during these winters to Washington. Henri de Regnier, the poet, and his wife, De Heredia's sister; Senator Lodge's poet son; Judge Berry, then in Washington, and Cambon himself made one very agreeable luncheon party. Madame de Regnier, who is a poet herself, and very striking in her exiguous Spanish type, wore rings on every finger of her restless little hands; De Regnier recounted his visit to Chicago, and said that he had been taken to the stockyards, that he had fainted on the raised wooden walks which spanned the great abattoir, and had been with difficulty saved from falling into the sea of blood and murder which seethed beneath him. Like a fevered dream of Vereschagin was that scene as I saw it myself a few years later, and strangely complete in the composition of its practical artificers, who, surely, had no idea of any artistic effect, however Avernian. The brutal blows of the executioner's hammer falling with a horrible rhythm upon each animal's skull as it was driven from the pen, the amazing rapidity of the dismemberment, the crowning central horror of the great electric light over the red pool with its surrounding rows of severed heads in regular arrangement, made in

191

my memory an ineffaceable and unsurpassed picture of horror often recalled, together with the impression it so inevitably produced upon the French poet in search of sensations in America. Murder, however humanitarian, was never so mathematically staged.

Edward Rod, the novelist, very conscientious and very Swiss, also lunched with me, and has left no recollections except his embarrassment at the presence of unaccustomed chocolate bonbons on my table which he attempted to negotiate with a fork.

The day when Paderewski and Saint-Gaudens lunched with me provided an eloquent duo of compliments from the greatest pianist to the greatest sculptor of their day, and a picture of strikingly beautiful faces, the Jovian type of the sculptor, the archangel head of the musician.

On another occasion, when Ysaye lunched with us, his gayety and good-fellowship rose to such a pitch that he could not keep his seat at table, but sprang to his feet as he related his anecdotes or broke into sparkling witticisms. His example was followed by each one of my guests, who took the floor one after the other to deliver their several contributions.

The embarrassment of M. Rod over unfamiliar American viands was shared by Humperdinck when he dined with me in New York. No less disturbed was his hostess, who could speak no German with the great composer, while he could speak neither English nor French. His neighbor at table, Mrs. Otto Kahn, was our interpreter, and it was she who encouraged him to try the succeeding dishes which were offered him. Soup he understood, fish mousse was a stranger which he declined, but with less fright than the dynamitic black mold of mushrooms, a triumph of my chef, which he waived away in unconcealed terror, exclaiming that "he had had quite enough" of stuffed capon. One might hope that the exquisite production of his "Koenig's Kinder," in which Geraldine Farrar was at her absolute best, at the Metropolitan Opera House, had shown this timid master that, although the food which was offered to him and the language he heard were terrifying, his music could be given in America quite as well as in his native land.

After one winter in 16th Street, near the White House, we leased another house farther up the same street, and there spent another winter so agreeably that we decided to make Washington our winter home. With this intention, we took on a long lease that house of General Meigs at the corner of Vermont Avenue and N Street which I had visited so often while the general was still living, and companioned his daughter, Mrs. Forbes. We greatly altered and beautified it, and when we came to live in its ample agreeable rooms we found that one of them, the general's old library, was large enough for weekly musical evenings. Several successful operas, such as "Foxy Quillor," and "The Highwayman," "Red Feather," and the "Golden Butterfly," were written and produced during these years. The first two were written for the comedian Jerome Sykes, whose success as the detective in the comedy rôles of these operas was very notable. In my opinion, the libretto of "The Highwayman" is the best Harry Smith ever wrote. The lyrics are of a very high order, and the humorous dialogue, so well rendered by Sykes, well up to any standard of comic opera. The operas, "Red Feather" and "The Golden Butterfly," were written for a well-known soprano, Grace Studdford, who carried them also to a success, both enduring, as did the Sykes operas, for more than four years.

My own literary efforts had resulted in the publishing of two novels. *A Sawdust Doll,* written in Lake Forest was a slight sketch of New York life. It had a certain success, being republished in England and even in India, and running through several editions. "How I wish," said my friend George Moore, when I saw him in London, when we had crossed the Atlantic for a summer in Europe—"how I wish I could have advised you while you were writing this book. It is very nearly good, your New York scenes are admirable, but your sentimental reflections are singularly young and very much interrupt the narrative." Any word of advice from this master of English was naturally authoritative, as I had found on another occasion, when I read to him a curiously unconstructed outpouring of feelings and opinions, young and inexperienced, and quite unworthy of publication. Our interview was in a bare hotel drawing-room in London, and as the last sheet fell on the floor, among the plentiful shower of cigarette ashes, I glanced at my patient auditor, and saw a flushed face and a distracted blond lock of hair standing up from his head in an unforgettable picture of discouragement. "Oh," he groaned, "it is so bad, so very bad, and yet it is beautifully written. What *have* you been try-

COACH WITH MR. McCREERY DRIVING
MRS. DE KOVEN NEXT

ing to say?" Needless to add that I gathered up my unlucky manuscript, and it rests in my strong box of papers, still retaining its cigarette ashes and with its rejected pages unrestored to their sequence.

By the Waters of Babylon was written amid many social occupations during the winter of 1901 in our second 16th Street (Washington) house, and brought me my first experience in the search for historical atmosphere. I dipped, all unconscious of the extent of the domain, into Assyriology in my efforts to learn something of Babylon and its Persian kings. My earnestness quite terrified Mr. Adler, then the curator of the Smithsonian Institution, who was a very respected authority on this period. "My God! she is serious!" I heard him whisper under his breath as I plied him with questions. With great patience he took several weeks, as he admitted, to prepare answers to some of them. As I reread this book, with its Babylonian cover depicting the towers of the city, I find it satisfactory in description and the evocation of the painted palaces, the rivers and walls and the burning desert, but wholly devoid of any adequate characterization of the persons of the story. The attempt to realize apparently living people in so distant and unfamiliar a period has failed in the hands of many writers, whose names I would not dare to mention. It was indeed far beyond my capacity, but the descriptive parts were praised in the critical reviews, and its dramatic possibilities, as I have related, very nearly attained to public and possibly successful recognition. However, after these two efforts I came to the conclusion that I did not

195

possess the authentic imagination of the novelist, did not experience that dramatic realization of character which was essential, and waited for another vehicle for my still unsatisfied desire to express myself and whatever ability I might possess.

Our stay in Washington was occupied by my husband's attempt to found in a city of winter residents a permanent orchestra. The too hopeful friend who suggested the idea to my husband was, after a year of not unhopeful results, deprived of her independent income, which was to subsidize the new orchestra. Many distinguished soloists appeared under my husband's baton, and, like Paderewski, enthusiastically recognized his capabilities as a conductor.

After McKinley's assassination and the accession of Roosevelt to the Presidency, a far greater social activity prevailed at the White House. The presence of Roosevelt's dominating personality was an element of continued interest. Anecdotes repeated first hand regaled many dinner tables and favored friends assumed attitudes of importance. The program of entertaining was taken in hand by the President's sister and Mrs. Lodge, and all available evenings during the season were assigned to those hostesses of the Cabinet and the Senate who were considered worthy by these all-powerful ladies. The guests, also, were definitely restricted to those of their choice. The result was so deplored by one Senator, who had sat as many as thirty times in one winter by one of these ladies, that he protested and finally succeeded in enlarging the so narrowly restricted lists of guests.

There was, in truth, something not quite consistent with the customs and principles of a republic in this dictation, something very nearly royal in its assumption of authority in matters social, and this dictation restricted the variety and interest which our legislators had been accustomed to find in their hours of relaxation. The effort to make Washington a chamber of so few stars has not been repeated.

The habit of living in the White House tends inevitably to the assumption of divine appointment. This tendency, which was witnessed in the Roosevelt régime, had been seen before in that of General Grant. It is in itself a clear indication that the unwritten law that a third term is not to be demanded of the suffrages of the people is a wise one. If it is true that one member of the Roosevelt family commanded a Cabinet lady to rise in the presence of one of the young princes of the White House, it was no more expressive of this attitude of permanent possession of supreme authority than Roosevelt's own address to an audience, during that last desperate Progressive campaign, as "my people." Megalomania, in the persons of Roosevelt, Wilson, and the Kaiser has been the ruling force back of the world conflict, activating and intensifying all economic and racial jealousies. The conviction that in his wisdom alone was to be found the welfare of the American people for a time obscured Roosevelt's loyalty to the party which had raised him to leadership and opened the way to his defeat and to Wilson. And Wilson himself exemplified to an even greater degree the delusion of autocratic privilege and destiny.

One of the secrets of what has been called Wilson's "intellectual dishonesty" has escaped the attention of the many analysts of his character. That secret is to be found in his Southern birth. Although now recovering something of its ancient prosperity. the South, for the period of two generations, had been oppressed by the weight of poverty, of isolation from the rushing tide of prosperity which enriched the North, and of the cultivation which is the prize of prosperity. Under these restricting conditions a hatred of the successful North, a contempt of the so-called plutocracy, was as inevitable a Southern heritage as poverty and ignorance themselves. The mind which essays to pierce through this double weight must be like a rapier for keenness and like a rapier, quick and subtle. That *"perfervidum ingenium Scotorum"* of Alexander Hamilton, of Paul Jones, and of Albert Beveridge was also Wilson's birth inheritance, his birthplace, a little half-forgotten town in the ruinous South. An intellect of high, but by no means of wide perceptions, was vitalized and intensified by an ambition, half vindicative, against anything which wore the robe of opulence, and wholly egotistic.

I once heard Mr. Hughes say that all Americans should be grateful to Wilson because he had expressed the idealism of our country. The perfection of phrase to which he had undoubtedly attained was the ambition of those early years when a vision of the future must have haunted his dreams with that curious foreknowledge often seen in predestined rulers. For not only did the young Wilson dream of an executive power which would override the Constitution, but to wing his words

House on the Thames

with an eloquence which, according to his own prophecy, might have national and even international influence, he commanded that for an hour each day pages from the Bible, from Shakespeare and Demosthenes should be read to him.

No idealistic dreams could command the support which was needful for their realization, when so nullified by the pride and isolation of Wilson's peculiar type of megalomania. And affection, human sympathy, added no lubricating oil to this world machine of pre-destined glory and of failure. Roosevelt, whom to know was to love, in spite of vanities and their accompanying resentments, the *revers de medaille* of all highly developed egoisms, was a man whose like we shall never again see, a patriot and an inspiring influence and memory in his beloved country.

But as I saw him, just arrived at the pinnacle, young and abounding in vigor as he entered the House of Representatives to deliver his eulogy on McKinley, I was frightened. His attitude spoke too clearly of pride, his stride was too conquering. In that hint of the superman there was danger, as the event declared.

During his first administration his enthusiasm was still guided by the remarkable McKinley Cabinet and Hay and Root were still by his side. It was my privilege to know both these able defenders of every wise measure, these examples of brilliant powers, wholly dedicated to the best administration of their responsibilities.

John Hay was, with Lodge, a very notable type of literary statesman, rare in our country and the glory of

England. In his association with Lincoln as his secretary, John Hay alone, among American politicians, had precisely the training for a public life which is often sought for in England. His journalistic experiences with Horace Greely and Whitelaw Reid in the New York *Tribune* increased his knowledge of men and affairs and did not spoil his delightful poetic gift, whose expression, though not large in volume, has so perfectly preserved the note of American humor. A nicety in literary phrase may have its great political value, as was demonstrated in Hay's state papers, which defined the essential rights of China, when its "administrative entity" was threatened by the predatory powers. This was an illustration of the power of the long arm of circumstance, the circumstance being Hay's expert use of English, and its derivation long ago as a youth in the newspaper office of the New York *Tribune*. And John Hay was as ardent a poet in life as Roosevelt himself, although far less robust in his expression of the enjoyment. Friendships with him, as with so many *esprits d'élite,* were romances; the cult of a mind which set no limits to human affections. To the end of his life in Washington, the daily walk with Henry Adams was a peripatetic ritual, sacredly observed. And even amid the anxieties and preoccupations of his overtaxed existence, he had time to write poems which have the fragile, although luxurious, bloom of autumn roses. Mr. Hay and Henry Adams built their houses next each other on the corner of that broad street, which an enthusiastic Washington lady wished to rename the Avenue of the Presidents. This avenue leads from the White House

200

out to the country, past many of the embassies, and along its sunny pavements Hay and Adams have been seen by the sympathetic Washington public, walking and talking, during many years of enviable companionship. Cabot Lodge was the third member of this political-literary triumvirate. But in Henry Adams's house was established a *cenacle* of exclusive choice, as ardent in devotion to its patron saint, "Uncle Henry," as the Capitoline matrons and virgins of the Roman decadence were to Marcella. I was never a member of this enviable band of happy devotees, but I like to remember that in the last summer of his life Mr. Adams spoke to me, from a group of his friends, on the porch of a golf club near Boston, saying, "Your next subject, Mrs. de Koven, is . . ."

I had not been informed that Mr. Adams had read my *Biography of Paul Jones,* but was astonished that he should have chosen precisely the individual in our history whose life I had been contemplating as the object of my investigation. I also thought it a remarkable example of his appreciation and his kindly interest, particularly as some hitherto unrecorded inconsistencies in the career and character of his celebrated progenitor had not been overlooked in my *Biography.*

I knew Charles Francis Adams far more intimately than his brother, the adored "Uncle Henry" of the Washington *cenacle,* and I can hear now the chuckle with which he threw himself back in his chair as he sat, under the October sunshine, in that delightful meeting-place of all Americans, Hot Springs, Virginia. I had asked him if there were any reference to Paul Jones in his great-grandfather's unpublished papers.

"John Adams never made any reference to your hero," he replied.

"But did you not know that the most vivid personal description of Paul Jones in existence was written by him?"

This was the reason for his chuckle of delight at his own mistake and the expression of the Adams humor, which in his redoubtable ancestor, was obscured by what he himself called his "terrible vanity."

If John Hay brought much enthusiasm to his friendships, his delight in the nearer relations of his family was even more intense. I remember one day in London, when he was ambassador, he showed me a sonnet by his daughter. His pleasure was expressed in a chuckle as merry as that of Mr. Adams, over its polished phrases.

"I could not have written that myself," he declared, as he put the little poem in his pocket and turned to greet the crowd of American visitors in his drawing-room.

Mrs. Hay had a serene and classic beauty, and, if the truth must be told, had rather less than the ordinary amount of American versatility and gayety of manner.

As long ago as the year 1884, on my wedding journey, I met that Clarence King who was the idolized friend of both Hay and Adams. An example of his wit, of which Adams has left so enthusiastic a record, was expressed in his reply to a remark of my own about Mrs. Hay, during one of our steamer-rail conversations. I had discussed the influence of a hostess upon every corner of her house and upon each visitor, and had remarked that Mrs. Hay's atmosphere was not stimulating.

"Atmosphere!" replied Mr. King. "She is not an atmosphere; she is a climate; and I might have murdered her, for she married my best friend."

Of Mr. Root I used often to hear from the enthusiastic narratives of his subordinate in the War Department, General Clarence Edwards. General Edwards was the head of the actual Colonial Bureau of that Department, during the first years of our possession of the Philippine Islands. His natural pride in the officials and the measures which at that time were so successfully demonstrating our national possibilities as colonial administrators, rose to a lyrical pitch when he spoke of Mr. Root.

"I have heard him dictate pages of the most intricate and critically important dispatches without any previous preparation and without the change of a word." The dispatches were to the Vatican when the Jesuits needed repression in Manila. "There never was so clear a mind," General Edwards said, "or such a memory."

It is not possible to write of Washington during my residence there without speaking of Mary Patten and her sisters. Their birth was Irish and their solidarity was like that of all Irish, away from Ireland. Their father found his fortune in the far West, as did John Mackay, Mills, and Fair. Their mother was pretty, ambitious, and clever—clever enough to send her brood of girls to a convent in Paris and then to bring them to Washington.

There, it is said, they first talked, unintroduced, on the street corners, to diplomatic new arrivals, who found them immensely diverting. Thereafter within the hitherto closed doors of the Washington residents they very soon proceeded. The next step was the establishment of what in diplomatic language was called the "Irish Legation." I could not count the dinners I have attended when Mary Patten's audacious comments upon political measures (for audacity was the larger part of her wit) set the authors of those measures into roars of laughter.

During these years, which were otherwise exceedingly gay and full of amusement, my husband struggled heroically to save the cause of the orchestra. The last and determining blow, which finally emptied the audience hall, was the choice of the President's wife of the orchestra afternoons for the White House receptions. Tea in Washington was more appreciated than music, although it was so plentiful and music so rare. The effort to continue the orchestra without the promised financial subsidy was finally very harmful to my husband's health and diminished the vitality necessary for the writing of his operas. This interlude of misfortune was accompanied also by a serious illness of my own, which compelled me to spend the summer in Canada and to abandon the house we had rented in Newport for the season of 1902. I was able to return for the winter 1902-03, but the disappointment regarding the orchestra finally decided us to return to New York and look after our theatrical fences.

One recollection concerning the orchestra is very agreeable. It was on the occasion when it was Mr. Roosevelt's wish that my husband should bring the orchestra to play at the White House. The orchestra was in its place and the Red Room crowded when the President appeared at the door. He paused a moment while his eye swept the room, when, descrying me in my place, he immediately found a seat beside me. His comments upon the music displayed the remarkable variety of his appreciations. When I attempted to express my own appreciation of his compliment by saying that I was glad that my husband had been able to contribute an hour of pleasure to his own happy days, he replied: "Why, how nicely you say it! Yes, my days are happy, very happy."

Of the happiness of his life our great President has left a record which in my humble opinion is his best legacy to his country. In the letters to his children, fortunately collected by a discriminating friend and published after his death, Roosevelt has left a story of that same romantic love of his family which was expressed in the letters of Mrs. Blaine. In the intense interest and sympathy with each and every one of his children, his comprehension of their different characters, his advice regarding their occupations and their possible development, he showed himself the ideal father and friend.

And as for that beloved comradeship with his wife, how can one read of the hour which he dedicated each day to her, when together they would sit in the lovely White House gardens, in the companionship of birds and flowers, without a thrill of tender sympathy with a heart endowed with the best gift of all? How can one fail to praise the gratitude and the wisdom which could turn aside from all his occupations to savor this gift to the full? In an old Italian garden, once the beloved retreat of Lorenzo, the Medici poet, is a monument wreathed in carved flowers and half hidden in the bird-haunted wood. "Birds and flowers," runs the inscription, "give a crystalline mood." This was the mood of Roosevelt's happiest hours and a precious memory in the hearts of a grateful people.

CHAPTER FIFTEEN

IN the summer of 1903 my father's illness deeply clouded my annual visit to Lake Forest, and on September 23 his long life of eighty years came to its end. A halo of autumn, golden by day, pure silver by night, hung over the painted forest and over the lake. The silence, the peace, and the glory of nature fulfilled and perfected, pervaded the wooded aisles of our beloved home and an incense of blessing seemed to enfold us with its promise of life recurring, ever renewed. Love and praise of the noble life which had blessed us so long brought us tender comfort from old friends and servants. For twenty-five years our gardener had made our "Fair Lawn" beautiful, and none of the tributes to our father so touched us as the sight of his tears as he wove a garland of ivy, "a last service to the best man I have ever known."

In the period of mourning after my father's death I began to dwell on the seedling idea which was destined to afford me the most satisfying occupation of my life. The wife of my father's old friend, Mr. Hitt, whom I encountered at Murray Bay, hoping to interest me in my illness, had given me a copy of A. C. Buell's *Life of Paul Jones*. I read it and found it as agreeable as my friend had promised, and then thought no more about it. But during the next winter she visited me in our Wash-

207

ington house and told me that certain love letters written to Jones, unidentified, and for the most part unpublished, existed in the Library of Congress. I was
then impressed with the idea that unpublished material
relating to a personality which at that time was very
widely discussed might be worth investigating. I found
them, those tear-stained, eloquent letters, and found
therein also so vivid a reflection of the charm of our
singularly romantic naval hero, that I proposed to Mr.
Charles Scribner, who had published Buell's biography, to write a story of Paul Jones's life at Paris and
Versailles at the time of his glory, the letters to be the
nucleus of the book. Mr. Scribner quite readily accepted my proposition. Then followed, first in Washington and then in Lake Forest, an examination of the
memoirs of the period. But when I attempted to locate
the authorities for Buell's facts, which I found in his
list of consulted books, I was confronted with the discovery that they were either non-existent or contained
no reference whatever to Jones. I should, of course,
except the biographies previous to Buell's and the standard histories. When in my perplexity I went in the
autumn to Washington, I was informed by Mr. Worth-
ington Ford, then head of the Manuscript Division of
the Congressional Library, that Buell had never consulted the Jones documents. I was also informed that
his own personal history was as questionable as his
authorities. I then very carefully perused the great
number of Jones's papers, which, originally bought by
Peter Force for his famous and unrivaled collection of
Revolutionary documents, had passed into the custody

Mrs. Reginald de Koven
WASHINGTON, 1897

Mrs. Reginald de Koven
HOMBURG, 1891

of the government Library. This search revealed such a mass of new material that I became convinced that the authoritative biography of the man whose initiative, advice, and brilliant exploits entitle him to be called the founder of the American navy, was yet to be written. Thus I was at last provided with a task for which I had no preparation, but which I believed I might accomplish with patience and conscientious study.

The discovery of new historical material in the silence of a library, a pleasure which was often mine during those long studious years, I have found equal to any delights I have ever experienced and quite as exciting. My discovery of Buell's quite unparalleled audacity in the fabrication of official documents and letters from our eminent forefathers was published in a page of the New York *Times*. I had waited to publish this *exposé* until my hero's body had been finally and formally received at Annapolis by a crowd of some 10,000 people, who had there assembled, and who listened to many eloquent speeches filled with quotations from Buell.

General Horace Porter, who had decried my investigations, approached me at Newport a few months after the appearance of this article, and although he had written a laudatory preface to a new edition of Buell, and quite naturally considered himself the sponsor of the hero, whose forgotten remains he had restored to his country, made a most gallant *amende* for his skepticism. He circled around me as I stood at the door of the Newport Casino, for several hesitating moments, and then, with his hat in his hand, he exclaimed: "It is only Paul

Jones dead which interests me. His life you may deal with as you please."

We were placed together at many dinners, in the years which followed our mutual attention to Paul Jones, but the heads thus placed in proximity never knocked together, and I was asked by the general, when attacked about the authenticity of Jones' body, for documents which did help him in his answers to a perennial Philadelphia objector, who had published his doubts about the mortal remains of our hero.

During eight years my principal occupation was the collecting of every published account of Jones, and of every unpublished and published letter in private and public collections, and the arrangement and final writing of the biography, which was at last published by Mr. Scribner himself, in the spring of 1913. It was sometimes a labor which tired me physically, but never wearied my mind or exhausted my interest. My *exposé* of Buell's forgery was never answered, and my book is used at Annapolis. When in a long article in the New York *Sun* the critic with a gesture of chivalric compliment admitted that the thousand pages of the book were justified, I felt and still feel great gratitude that this subject of significance in our history had so curiously fallen into my hands.

Mr. Barrett of the Pan-American Society, in relating a conversation with a group of his Washington naval friends, indicated the natural incredulity of the officers regarding my fitness to write this biography.

"I had a conversation about you last week in Washington," he said, "with five retired admirals. We were talking about your book, and they said you were a 'society lady' (!) and the wife of a composer of comic opera, but I told them that I knew you."

"I think you are telling me," I replied, "that no one of these retired admirals believed that I had written it."

"Well, madam," he admitted, "as a matter of fact, they didn't, but I bought five copies of the book for them and I think they will change their opinion."

Buell's book had been quoted widely in the public speeches of ambassadors and politicians, and had been also accepted without question, by the naval editor of the London *Times,* and by such journals as the *Spectator.* Mr. Thursfield of the *Times* made the Buell Paul Jones the subject of the principal essay in his book called *Nelson and other Naval Studies.* When challenged by me to examine his authorities, he replied in a letter to the *Times,* in which he informed his readers that he would investigate Mrs. de Koven's "allegations" and apprise them of the results. The replies he received from the Navy Department and that of the Manuscript Division of the Congressional Library, as well as the letter from the Rev. Cyrus Townsend Brady, author of an entirely correct little book about Jones, in the "Great Commander" series, were all turned over to me. Mr. Thursfield did not inform his readers directly that he was convinced of the truth of my "allegations," but in a review of my book, when it was published in England, he made a quite frank *amende,* in stating that my disclosure of Buell's inventions was of value to students of naval history.

When the national monument to Jones was about to

211

be erected in Washington, I was invited to inspect its design and to read the proposed inscription, which I found, to my natural indignation, was a perpetuation of one of the most striking of Buell's inventions. Mr. Padgett, the chairman of the marine committee, was the author of this inscription, and no documents from the Navy Department, which I duly presented to him, had the least effect upon his determination to put Buell's words in enduring stone, to the equally enduring ridicule of the government, upon the monument.

The committee appointed by Congress for the erection of the monument was, however, apprised just in time that my investigations should be heeded, and Mr. George Meyer, then Secretary of the Navy, informed me in my box at the opera in New York that his committee had eliminated the inscription. The monument itself was unveiled on a rainy day in April, 1913, and to the ceremony I was duly invited. On the little platform sat Mr. Meyer, the Secretary of the Navy, Admiral Dewey, and General Porter, and place was made for me among them, and thus I saw the soldiers and sailors marching in the rain to do honor to my hero. A little later, in a crypt at Annapolis, the much-traveled remains of Paul Jones found their final and glorious resting-place. In a simple and entirely truthful summary of his accomplishments, drawn up by Jones himself, is the phrase, "He hath made the flagg of America respected among the flaggs of other nations." No such glorious monuments as the crypt at Annapolis or the statue in Washington from the country which he had loved beyond any other visited his imagination when, broken with disappointment, horror-stricken at the anarchy of revolutionary France, he died, alone, in his little Paris lodging. A better recognition of his inspiring character than crypt or monument is the quotation from his own eloquent exposition of the ideals of a naval officer, which, posted at the head of each student's note book, is read every day in Annapolis.

For a number of years, even after I had disclosed the falsity of the document on the founding of the navy, which Buell ascribed to Jones, this was taught at Annapolis. This remarkable paper, including only one short quotation from one of Jones's letters, was declared by Mr. Thursfield of the London *Times* to be the "charter of Annapolis and far more important than any of the victories" of its supposed author. I have always held the opinion that Buell himself was not the author of this paper, but that he employed some anonymous and very excellent writer to contribute it to his pages. Buell's own journalistic style, for he was a journalist and loved a good story far too well, does not, in my opinion, appear in any phrase of this paper.

CHAPTER SIXTEEN

DURING the summer of 1905, passed at Lake Forest, my mother slowly faded, and two days after the anniversary of my father's death, in the same golden September weather, she closed her eyes upon life. Among all the gifts which she bestowed upon her children, none was so shining as the manner of her death. For months we realized that she had already passed the earthly bounds of the spirit and was dwelling in immortality. Clairvoyant in her perceptions, gracious, even witty, with her Puritan preoccupations quite forgotten, she left us unforgettable messages of wisdom and bade us good-by with a smile. Her last thoughts were of my father and she continually dwelt on the days of their youth, on that white silk high hat in which she had seen him as he trod the streets of little Chicago in the early days of their acquaintance. So they departed, our admirable parents, leaving us their standards, their high principles, and the memory of consistently noble lives and a peace and harmony never marred by one harsh word to each other or to ourselves.

The winter of 1905-06 was passed in New York in a little apartment on Madison Avenue, where I was deeply absorbed in the study of "Paul Jones" documents, and spent most of my time at the Public Library. This study was continued during our residence in the

214

ɴext house we took in New York at 42 East 66th Street, where we lived for five years. In the 66th Street house we continued the musical parties which we had begun at Irving Place, and then, although a new rule of the Metropolitan Opera House forbade its singers, without equal compensation with the terms of their contracts, to sing outside the Opera House, we found no such inhibition with Oscar Hammerstein's singers. In the large library at the back of the house I heard such thrilling music as haunts the ear of my memory, and must so linger in the ears of all who heard it. Mary Garden, Tetrazzini, Ancona, and McCormack, alone and in duets which shook the ceiling—altos and sopranos and 'cellists and violinists, as of old, contributed what were really feasts of music. Gilibert with his exquisite lyrical style, Cavalieri with her unequaled beauty, Maurice Renaud and Madame Schumann-Heink also continued the standards and traditions of the musical house it had been our opportunity and pleasure to establish.

And how generous were those musical friends of ours, coming from Philadelphia to sing for us, for love only, and on more than one occasion risking their contracts to please us! On one occasion, when fourteen friends only were assembled at our luncheon table, Renaud and Mary Garden, Schumann-Heink and Tetrazzini, all lent us their lovely voices; surely the stars sang together for that little party.

After two years at Bryn Mawr my daughter had been duly brought out first in Washington, then in Newport, in the summer of 1906, and we spent the succeeding

winters in New York, with summer intervals at Nauheim and finally at Bar Harbor. During the second
summer in Maine, in 1910, she became engaged to Hans
Kierstede Hudson, whose Kierstede ancestor was the
first surgeon in New Amsterdam. He married the
daughter of Anneke Yans, owner of that part of Man-
hattan which has been called Trinity Farm. Every day,
as my son-in-law makes his way to the Stock Exchange,
he passes the site of Anneke's farm, and each summer
day, in his house on Long Island, he looks on walls
painted with the houses and ships of his Dutch ancestors. He married my only child in the winter of 1911,
and in the spring my husband and I went to Switzerland for the summer.

The summers of 1911 and 1912 we spent at Vevey,
and passed long delightful days, in the house of Madame
Sembrich at Lausanne, with Ernest Schelling and his
wife at their lovely château at Garengo, with Josef
Hofmann and his wife at Mt. Pelerin, and with Paderewski and his wife at Morges. There Madame Sembrich sang my husband's songs to him, there two years
later we celebrated Paderewski's birthday, a very memorable one, on July 31, 1914. At Paderewski's house
also I met the Comtesse de Noailles, a diminutive Arabian type of extraordinary and haunting loveliness. I
heard, also, an example of her torrential eloquence, as
springing to her feet she discussed the character of the
Jewish race with Paderewski, also on his feet, in a duo
of excited argument. I was immensely interested to see
the greatest poet of France in such a mood and in such
company.

MRS. DE KOVEN IN A RUSSIAN COSTUME WORN AT THE BALL GIVEN BY MR. AND
MRS. DAVID JAYNE HILL IN WASHINGTON, 1898

Although, on returning to New York after our Washington residence, my husband had built the Lyric Theatre with the idea of providing a permanent house for his own and other comic operas, the lessees of the theater were sadly different from the old American managers who had played "Robin Hood" for so many successful years. A comment on the curiously hostile fate which followed the triumphant fortune of my husband's early productions is now inevitable. The Shubert brothers were three when my husband leased his theater to them, and Sam, the eldest, was kindly, human, and even artistic in his perceptions, and was very fond of my husband. Under his careful direction the first production in the theater, called "Happyland," with an adequate cast, including De Wolf Hopper, in a most amusing rôle, was eminently successful. And then Sam Shubert was killed in a railway accident. Again—and this was a blow of even greater misfortune—the librettist of "Happyland," Fred Ranken, whose charming lyrics and carefully constructed dialogue were very satisfactory to my husband, died of typhoid fever a few days after the production of this successful piece.

Harry Smith and my husband, after a long collaboration, had separated, and during many years my husband vainly sought for a libretto which could be a possible vehicle for his music. No care was shown by the remaining Shubert brothers, in assisting my husband's always lovely music, with casts whose ability might have carried to success the inadequate librettos, and so there were many disappointments and several failures, while "Robin Hood" still pursued, with various companies, its

217

career of success. At last the remarkable revival of this opera at the Knickerbocker Theatre intervened, to afford us a period of pleasure, and one of my happiest recollections is that of my husband's delight as he watched the performance of this opera, with its cast of Metropolitan singers. A company, bearing his own name, was soon after organized and managed by him. This company continued a successful existence for several years, with emoluments more than satisfactory to all concerned, except my husband, who was far too generous and too sensitive to qualify for a theatrical manager. Dishonesty also became a disastrous element among his subordinates, and I was distinctly pleased when it became apparent that a composer was by nature unfitted to be a manager.

In the last week of 1912 we took possession of our house on Park Avenue, in which was a room sufficiently large for the reception of the audiences of our friends whom we invited to hear the music so willingly contributed by those friends, the singers and instrumentalists who have for so many years honored us by their unexampled generosity. This house we opened on the last day of the year 1912. In tearing haste I myself superintended the last work of upholsterers, painters, and decorators, for Madame Sembrich, who wished an interval of rest before a concert on the coming 3d of January, refused to sing for us one day later than that New Year's eve of 1912. Neither architect nor decorators were present, and all day, from eight o'clock in the morning until nine in the evening, I stood on my feet, conducting what seemed a hopeless effort to prepare the

(*Above*) Bust of Reginald de Koven Made in Vevey, 1915
(*Below*) Mr. de Koven's Studio, 1025 Park Avenue

house for our guests. As the last sofa was wheeled into place and the last curtain was swept to the last window, the bell began to ring, with the coming of our audience, and as suddenly as a stage picture falls into place at the last moment before the curtain rises, so did my house, with its sixteenth-century rooms, assume an appearance of permanency, almost of accustomed familiarity and harmony. Madame Sembrich and Ernest Schelling came up the stairs hand in hand, with a charming friendliness, prepared, as they had so kindly proposed, to open our house for us. McCormack also, for the last time ignoring the protests of his managers, came also, to fill the new music room with his incomparable voice. And there was also a 'cellist, and Mr. Paul Rumers, who contributed his delightful lyrics to the concert. With its paneled walls, and its absence of any drapery to obstruct the voice, the room at this, its first trial as a hall of music, disclosed perfect acoustic properties. McCormack's voice floated out in all its purity, and he was so pleased that he approached me, saying, and even repeating: "I thought my voice was tired. Did it sound tired?" A temporary fatigue in the beautiful voice of the singer, who has since gathered his millions in his always thronged concerts, had in fact been apparent, but it is a pleasure to remember that the recovered fluency of its perfection was his experience in the last time he sang for us. It is also a pleasure to recall the approbation of my friends, who wrote many letters of praise of our new abode. Mrs. Fish enthusiastically wrote that it was a beautiful house and she was "glad we had it."

A costume ball, preceded by a quadrille of young dancers in Elizabethan costumes, was an appropriate function of this winter, with a long table covered with the viands of the period, and Elizabethan madrigals sung by a chorus from the musicians' gallery. A second winter of repeated musicales and occupations busy and agreeable we passed in our new house, and then we went to Europe.

CHAPTER SEVENTEEN

SWITZERLAND

THE shadow of my husband's illness, a hardening of the arteries, following many attacks of the gout, had begun to fall over our way, with occasional warnings, significant and terrifying. After a period in Nauheim, visits to Rome and Florence where we joined my sister, Mrs. Chatfield Taylor, and her husband, we went again to Vevey, and there the war enchained us for nearly two years. There was no war work for my husband's delicate health, and none of great utility for me, although I did what I could in the way of helping refugees and organizing entertainments for war sufferers, but we watched, as if from the stage box of Europe, the terrifying conflict, and sometimes even heard the echo of the guns over the Lake of Geneva, shrouded in a perpetual mist, and reflecting no longer the serenity of heaven in the white wonder of its surrounding heights, but the grief of the world. There, however, after my husband had slowly recovered from a dangerous illness, he began to compose an opera, commissioned by the Metropolitan Company, a work of greater seriousness than he had ever attempted. The libretto was adapted from the dramatic poem by Percy Mackaye, "The Canterbury Pilgrims." I had myself proposed this poem to my husband, thinking that the English subject might prove sympathetic to his lyric gift. Thus during our

221

stay in Vevey he was occupied in its composition. When the *triste* winter months had slowly passed by and sunlight and moonlight again illumined the lake, his recovered health and his joy in his work again brought us many days of contentment. By the flooding moonlight which filled our rooms I have heard the lovely lyrics, so perfectly expressing the unearthly love of the poet for his lady of dreams, well up from the melody-haunted soul of my musician, in hours of happy inspiration, happy in memory. I also found a subject to occupy my many hours of leisure in the history of the counts of Gruyère. This was written in English and translated into French, in which version it was published in Geneva. In a patois expressive as that of Provence, of the similar race inheritance which made southern France Celtic, Roman, and Burgundian, I found a very mine of story and ballad, and in that little country, hid away in the mountains, an astonishing survival of Celtic customs, for the early Helvetians were Celts. The wit, called Vaudois, from one of the cantons, in its purely Celtic character, although spoken in what is nearly Provençal, is also very nearly Irish. The ancient abode of the Gruyère counts is a unique scene of beauty, set on a hill looking up to the Oberland Mountains, and with its fortified houses surrounding the square of the high pitched tower, a vignette of almost theatrical composition. I was led very far in my study of the history of this pearl of Switzerland's beauty, little imagining that its perfection was the result of so many centuries and so remotely born in the past. Race characteristics and their persistency arrested my observation, and the ex-

amples I saw in my many journeys to the Gruyère valley and to the city on the hill astonished and delighted
my curiosity. A Burgundian warrior, tall as the skele-
tons in the Lausanne cathedral, one day worked at the
roadside; two classic dark beauties, with the closely
waved hair of the Roman marbles, sat sewing before
their cottages; and a group of blue-eyed girls, with the
laughing whimsical faces of Celtic Ireland, ran out of a
tobacco factory. Celtic wreaths still deck the deep
carved doorways of Gruyère—and not yet have they
forgotten the songs and the *coraules* of their cousins of
Brittany. Druid stones lie half hidden among the
mountains, and legends of sprites and May maidens still
haunt their streams and their caves, as in druid
Ireland.

In a life so simplified as it was at Vevey during those
two war winters, we found the contentment of our uninterrupted work, and a companionship far less interrupted than fell to our lot in busy New York. Many
of the exiled members of the societies of Europe,
dejecta membra indeed of falling dynasties, found
refuge in Switzerland during those years, and our
friends and acquaintances, with titles to conjure with,
played bridge with us for the most part very amiably,
in spite of very differing sympathies.

But by the middle of the second winter of the war,
and after my husband's opera was finished and my book
published, we determined to leave Switzerland, and on
our way toward home took a motor, and with two
friends made a trip from Aix-les-Bains through Provence to Nice. Through the mountains of Savoy, clearly

drawn as in an etching—black, blue, and brown—under the winter skies, we passed on our southern journey. Lyons, filled with the horror-stricken, mutilated youth of France, gave us a picture of war's cruelty. Grignan, overlooking the wide outspread plains, recalled Madame de Sévigné, and then we rolled through the classic wonders of Provence and saw Nîmes and Arles and Narbonne. A week's stop at Avignon, a visit to Les Baux, a night at Albé to see its fortlike cathedral by the red flowing stream, and its Venetian canal, and we also saw Carcassonne and Toulouse, and the walled city of Aigues les Mortes, whence St. Louis sailed for the Crusades. A brief stay at Monte Carlo brought us into the company of many old friends, whose presence was a helpful interlude to the strict and overcast war atmosphere of our quiet years in Switzerland. We had almost forgotten how to smile or be gay. At the station in Nice where we started on our way to Paris we saw, just drawing out, on another track, a long train of soldiers bound for Verdun. No less mad with war excitement than the one-legged soldier we had heard singing in the streets of Nice, these predestined victims of the Verdun holocaust were shouting *"tue tête"* in a chorus of joy. Joy and excitement were also in the expression of the splendid young French officer who gladly gave his seat to me to stand talking with a gray-bearded general in the corridor all through the night.

In Paris, as I walked with M. de Fouquières, of the Protocol, he remarked with pride upon the quiet aspect of the streets, the business traffic proceeding stoically enough during that breathless crisis of war.

COSTUME BALL, PARI

Koven Mansion

Uninformed by one of our motor party, who met us again in Paris, that the English Embassy had issued a warning to its nationals to avoid the Channel, in view of the new submarine menace to its waters, this friend bade us good-by with ill-concealed emotion. So we proceeded to Boulogne and boarded the little *Sussex*. Our cabin was in that fore part of the vessel which was later blown away by a torpedo. I asked vainly for three life belts for my husband, myself, and the friend who was returning to America with us, and only procured two of quite antiquated type. No preparations, apparently, had been made for the too likely disaster. But our journey was as rapid as the boat was capable of making, and the whistle which called the officers precipitately on deck was the only signal, from a sentinel fishing smack, that it was safe to enter the harbor. So Reginald de Koven, bringing his score of "The Canterbury Pilgrims" for performance in New York, was borne in safety to his destination, when Granados, returning only a week later, on the same boat, with fame and fortune finally attained, went down in its wreck. When we dined with Mr. Page in London, he told us how anxious he had been about us, how relieved he was to welcome us in England. It is one of my cherished memories to have known our great ambassador not only at this time in London, but at the very first moment of his accession to the wholly unexpected honor of the British mission. This first meeting was in the spring of 1913, in the house of my husband's cousins, Mr. and Mrs. Henry White, with whom I was stopping in Washington. At the luncheon table were Mr. and Mrs. Page, Mr. Wallace

225

and his wife—a daughter of Judge Fuller, whom my own father had recommended as Chief Justice to Cleveland—and also Mrs. House. I take no credit whatsoever at immediately recognizing the force, the humanity, and the eloquence which I found in Walter Page, but I do recall with pleasure the simple frankness of his conversation, his admitted surprise at his appointment, which he declared was like a "convulsion of nature." Wilson, the lately appointed Secretary of Agriculture, he said, was as ignorant of his new duties as himself. "We will just have to learn," he declared. After the departure of their guests Mr. and Mrs. White invited me to sit down and talk about "the Pages." "A great success," they both prophesied for the new ambassador and his wife. Mrs. Page's simplicity of dress and manner they said would be immensely sympathetic to the English. The success which their experience of England foresaw fulfilled their expectations, as all the world knows. Mr. Page's forecast of our own country's increased importance and influence, when he discussed it with me in London in 1916, proved him no less a prophet than Mr. White. "You will find it more interesting to live in America after the war," he said, "than anywhere in Europe." Mrs. Page, forgetting her great position, was sweetly pleased to make to me quite the most generous compliment regarding my husband and myself which I have ever received, on the day I found her in her house in London, surrounded by a number of the great ladies of England, who had quite clearly given her exactly the appreciation which Mrs. White had foretold. As to her simplicity and kindness, upon which

Mrs. White had based her *précis* of Mrs. Page, it is a pleasure to recall that Henry James found therein his best repose and comfort in the last days of his life in her company. That company, according to Mr. Page's published letter from the sanatorium, where he went in his vain effort to recover his health, "was so monstrous good" that he wished only for its delight, for its life-long support.

After the short interval in London we went to Falmouth to await the *New Amsterdam,* on which we were to brave the submarine on our homeward journey. No rooms were to be had except in a direly uncomfortable little boarding-house before which the guard, who were watching for air attacks, patrolled all through the night. There was much difficulty in securing sailors to man our ship, and as we stood on the dock on the morning we were to sail, we were told of the torpedoing of the *Sussex.* Beside us, as we received this news, was a former yachtsman of Falmouth, who pointed to the harbor, which had been emptied of everything which could sail to guard the *New Amsterdam* on her outward journey. This same yachtsman, whose duty had given him a varied experience with submarines, instructed us at the last moment as to the best method of jumping overboard. But we passed the Scilly Isles, scene of a late submarine disaster, in safety, and with a final sigh of relief saw them fade into the distance.

CHAPTER EIGHTEEN

THE next chapter was all of our recovered joy at being once more at home, although we did not return to our New York house in that late spring season. Soon we went to Boston in the wake of the Metropolitan Opera Company, so that my husband could play the score of "The Canterbury Pilgrims" to Mr. Gatti Cassazza's advisers, Mr. Setti, chorus master, and Mr. Romei, who occupied the position, without portfolio, of Gatti's musical conscience. It is a fact, remembered by many who were *au courant* with the negotiations which brought Gatti and Toscanini from the Scala to manage the New York Opera House, that the presence and assistance of the latter were the condition of the former's acceptance of the position he has occupied for so many years. Our experience with Mr. Gatti illumined the reasons for this condition. Endowed with great executive ability and a mechanical engineering talent, first demonstrated in his connection with music by his invention of a very successful *appareil* for the ride of the Valkyrs at the Scala, Mr. Gatti was launched into the career of *entrepreneur*. Mr. Gatti's musical perception was no greater, however, than that possessed by most Italians. This was the reason for the presence of Mr. Toscanini practically as co-manager, and he was the needful musical adviser and also the incomparable

228

conductor up to the time when his quarrel with the titular *entrepreneur* of the Opera House brought about his retirement. Mr. Romei then took the place of musical adviser. When Mr. Gatti, at Mr. Kahn's direction, journeyed to Vevey to hear the music of "The Canterbury Pilgrims," we were left in strange doubt as to the result of that hearing in spite of Mr. Gatti's reiterated statement of his own satisfaction. On our return to New York, Mr. Otto Kahn, who had not only commissioned the writing of the opera but had, by letter, promised its production, bringing us at an exceeding dangerous moment across the ocean, was almost disconcertingly reserved in our brief interview. All reasons for doubt, all hesitation as to the production of the opera, were cleared away in the meeting with Mr. Gatti's advisers in Boston. In a room at the Copley Plaza (while Mr. Gatti sat silent on the sofa) Mr. Setti and Mr. Romei followed my husband's playing of the opera with the orchestra score before them. It is a pleasure to recall that April morning when words of enthusiastic praise burst from the lips of those arbiters of our destiny, and a greater to remember that the contract for the production of the opera was signed the next day.

The summer which followed this safe return to our own country and this happy resolution of our operatic complications was a very pleasant one. On the North Shore near Boston, at Beverly, we took a charming house, belonging to Mr. Amos Lawrence, set among thick groves of evergreens, with a brook winding beneath their shade and a lovely garden. Summer Boston, scattered along the lovely North Shore, was very kind to us. My daughter and my enchanting three-year-old grandson were with us, and a musical cousin of my husband's. In the long summer days, as our little imp of joy and good comradeship delighted us with his play, his little speeches and comic verses, we spent many delicious hours. A hint of my husband's physical weakness I noted with a fear which I tried to suppress, when, on a return from his daily ride, I saw a pale face, and riding boots ominously relegated to the closet. This summer with its definite promise of the public production was happy because of that prospect. New York during the winter of 1917 was not our New York, as everyone was preoccupied with the war. I attempted to do war work myself, and gave a dramatic entertainment at my house for the benefit of Lady Johnstone's hospital in France, but the interest of the rehearsals of my husband's opera naturally occupied us. To the final dress rehearsal with costumes and scenery I went with Paderewski and his wife. Among all the recollections of friendship and sympathy which my memory holds of Paderewski, those hours by his side as he listened to my husband's music are the most precious. Its youthfulness, almost as gay as that of "Robin Hood," was commented upon by our friend, as well as its "lyrical genius" (for that was his expression), among other commendations of the orchestra treatment. Then on the 7th of March the great production arrived. We occupied a box just opposite the stage, surrounded in the adjoining boxes by many friends whose faces of happy satisfaction I watched while I followed also the succeeding acts and the growing enthusiasm of the vast

Left to right: PADEREWSKI, M. GAIFFE, OWNER OF THE CHÂTEAU D'ARIO, MADAME SEMBRICH, MRS. SCHELLING, DOCTOR STENGEL, MR. DE KOVEN, MR. SCHELLING

theater. The success, for it was success, and the only one of an American grand opera, was unquestioned. It was given very fair treatment by my husband's *confrères,* the critics, and supported by public interest in large audiences. But a curious fate decreed that in this opera my husband was to be another war victim, and to take his own tragic share in the world disaster. At the third performance, that memorable 17th of March, fluttering newspaper sheets made their appearance in the boxes below among the audience. Then in the midst of the murmur of voices Mr. Gerard rose from his seat in his box and announced that the President had requested the Congress to declare war against Germany. No one of that great audience, which instantly broke into a tumult of acclamation at this long-desired announcement, will ever forget the historical scene. Bodansky, the Austrian, strangely different from the sensitive swaying conductor his audiences have so often seen, rose in his seat and with a proud and immovable dignity led the orchestra as it played our National Anthem. The great theater echoed to the tumult of shouts and accompanying voices. The die was cast and our country was at war. When the curtain went up for the final act, the theater relapsed into comparative silence, but it was a silence full of suppressed murmurs from an inevitably preoccupied and inattentive audience. In the midst of the performance of the fourth act, Madame Ober, the principal woman, and the baritone also, fainted and were carried from the stage; they were both Germans, and this was their uncontrollable expression of emotion at the declaration of war against their country.

No hint that this remarkable incident was to involve the fate of his opera disturbed my husband during the summer of 1917. Always a determined advocate of American music, he made a gallant attempt to organize a national American opera company, with such encouragement from capitalists and musicians and such promised co-operation from the many musical organizations of our country that, except for the prevailing absorption in war preparations, he might have added this accomplishment to his career. In spite of this disappointment we passed a happy summer in a pretty house on the North Shore near the Essex Golf Club. There in a golden October, with two guests, we spent the last happy weeks of our lives. My husband was again composing and I was beginning another book. Thus we spent our mornings at work and our afternoons on the golf course, in an interval of peace and contentment. On our return to New York in November my husband was told that the management of the Metropolitan Opera Company had been so satisfied by the approbation of the public, so encouraged by the financial success of the "Canterbury Pilgrims," that it was to be given five more performances. This announcement, which meant that the opera had been included in the *répertoire* of the company, was a unique honor for an American work and brought its due satisfaction, but significant as the fact must always remain with those who knew of it, it was my husband's unhappy destiny to see its significance nullified by the event. The directing stockholders of the Metropolitan Company, remembering the public demonstration of the anti-American sympathizers with the German singers on the occasion of the announcement of war in the Opera House, demanded their dismissal. Mr. Gatti was so angry at this, to him, unique interference of the stockholders, that he refused to reassemble a cast, which had been still further diminished by the retirement of the principal soprano. And so the "Canterbury Pilgrims," successful by public and critical approval, was withdrawn from the stage.

My husband's desire to spend his summers nearer to New York than Newport or Bar Harbor was the reason for our sojourn on the North Shore of Massachusetts, first at Beverly, then at Manchester, and finally at Nahant. Thus of Boston and the Bostonians I have had considerable acquaintance. As I am myself of the very stock from which these New Englanders are derived, I felt many stirrings, and at times many harmonies, in this blood relationship. The daily drives through the avenues, shaded by the great elms of the region, the sight of the little towns of our sailor merchants with their beautifully preserved Georgian houses, gave me the authentic thrill of things already known, as if my own forefathers were articulate in my consciousness. Did I come upon that quality, sometimes called provincial, in the inhabitants of the province of Winthrop and the Puritans? I should not use the word provincial for the prevailing quality I found among them. I should use the word involution for the psychology of those self-inclosed and certainly self-sufficient Anglo-Americans. For the process of evolution which had its flowering in the crown, not of wild olives, but of sweetest lyrical bloom, of which Holmes and Longfellow and Bryant and Lowell were the ultimate expressions, has returned upon itself, and with a narrowing swirl of descending motion become involution. In this process the humanities have become antipathies, sympathy has been unhappily transformed into prejudice, and the rhythm of thought has resolved itself into short vibrations, restricted to personal interests. The theocracy of Winthrop has lost its religious fervor, and the rule of the "close corporation" which now is Boston is that of the family. Boston society is indeed a patriarchal institution. The sense of intimacy, of assured loyalty to no matter what expression of dependent or independent character or activity, is shown by the members of this institution and are its principal advantages. The outsider must expect to be rigorously examined as to his or her qualifications for acceptance in this intimacy. Motives and actions, innocent in themselves, may be condemned simply because they may differ from those of the members of this hierarchy, and if the test of similarity is not successfully sustained a shower of stones may drive away the intruder. A remarkable satisfaction with the conditions and privileges of this Boston family party prevails among all its members. I once heard from the lips of one of them the avowal that, as her friend So-and-so lived just opposite and her other preferred friend was on an adjacent corner, she had never seen any reason why she should go elsewhere, either to New York or to Europe, as she found herself placed in the center of the best society in the world.

Another indication of this unquestioning belief in the superiority of Boston over all the remainder of civilized creation was contained in the remark: "That girl's mother does not realize that she may at any moment ascend the pinnacle of American society. —— is really devoted to her."

"Who is ——?" was the reply which I, unaware of the name or qualifications of this crown prince of the blood royal of Boston, made to this statement. But my ignorance only argued my own barbaric exile from Athenian circles and their privileges.

No visitor to Boston or its environs could, however, fail to recognize the likeness in many important traits of the New Englanders to those of the English themselves.

Simplicity, self-respect, fidelity to friendship, independence of other standards, and a slow comprehension of those who represent those standards are all English traits and are all possessed by the new English of the Atlantic coast. Singly and away from Boston, they still prefer association with their own order, but are less militant toward the stranger. Privilege to deny all Puritan inheritances they often assume, but never fail of support by the other members of their hierarchy. But although restricted in sympathy, contented with their fortunate origin and associations, there are among the Bostonians numberless examples of excellent breeding, and often there appear very beautiful physical types, representing a long descended and gentle inheritance. I think it a privilege to have known them so well and to have received from them so many kindnesses. Even if, like many other visitors, I was made to realize

235

that a stranger, although enthusiastically received, should never dare to hope to be really a Bostonian.

They are very enviable folks, our New England cousins, and if by reason of separation from Boston itself we, their blood relatives, are made to feel that we have lost the precious place in their family circle, we are none the less New Englanders and understand them better than they understand us. The attitude of the English toward the American Colonists is in fact precisely similar to that of the New Englanders to the apostate Colonists of the Western states. Vigor of thought, independence of action, high loyalty to civic responsibilities are still active in Boston, and there are many examples of highly developed intelligence and character.

And Boston contained, until lately, the Isabella D'Este of modern times and the most vigorous and original poet of the present day in America. I was asked, a few years ago, to a small luncheon party including, besides my kind hostess, only Mrs. Gardner and Miss Lowell. Mrs. Gardner was, as is well known, no Bostonian by birth, while Miss Lowell was of the innermost circle. Independence of all manifestations of exclusiveness was Mrs. Gardner's attitude when by marriage she became a Bostonian, and through her long life of a great æsthete, if her incomparable collection of art merits for her the name, she astonished and finally dominated Boston. Her friends were selected with the same accurate attributions which made her unique collections, so that she made an illuminated center within the confines of derivative Puritanism, as closely

LIBRARY IN NEW YORK HOUSE

guarded and as warmly fragrant as the flowering pink-
walled courtyard of her palace of art. I knew this lute-
voiced lady while she was in the prime of her compelling
vitality. I was, as I remember, surprised that a face
singularly undistinguished, either by beauty or by any
mark of her original character, should be her outward
expression. Sloping shoulders like those of the Em-
press Eugènie and a small and beautifully proportioned
body were hers. Her dress, fantastically contrived with
priceless jewels set freakishly on the top of her small
ears or pinned like lanterns through a hayrick mop of
hair, arrested attention, like the rubies on her slippers
in Sargent's portrait. No personal deprivation or
effort was spared by Mrs. Gardner to complete her
great collection or to perfect the unique setting which
was to be her monument and her gift to Boston. In-
viting me once to a symphony concert, she apologized
for not providing a carriage to take me back to my hotel.
"I must leave you now," she said, "for it is the day when
I open my palace, and there is no one but myself to take
off the overshoes of my visitors." She lived alone with
one servant in her rooms at the top of Fenway Court,
and paid the price of Raphaels and Botticellis without a
murmur of her personal discomfort.

An ardor in her chosen ambitions, equal to that of
Mrs. Gardner, characterized Miss Lowell. With all her
individuality, Mrs. Gardner was not eccentric, except
by deliberate intention. Miss Lowell, of undiluted
Massachusetts blood, was an example, such as old England produces, of great eccentricity. She disdained to
concern herself about her great and increasing bulk of

body, with its dangerous threat to her life; she ignored the ordinary habits of existence and turned night into day, while from sunset to sunrise she worked as in a laboratory over her poems. At last the tireless chemist manipulated her talent into a new form of poetry, clear cut as a gem, fervid as flame, imaginative as a dream of the Orient, and endowed literature and life itself with new visions and new appreciations of beauty. From her first audacity and crudeness, which evoked more than one laughing and skeptical commentary from her contemporaries, she strove, and at last attained to the mastery of her material and the evolution of a new form of literary art. Did the hostile criticisms of the English authorities and students of Keats excite a dangerous resentment in this ardent biographer of the poet of England? Her death sadly and immediately followed this shock to the justifiable pride in her attainments. Surely it was unnecessary for the reviewer of the London *Times* to use the word "provincial" regarding Miss Lowell, not once, but again and again in his review of her book. It is my pleasure to recall an evening at her house in Brookline and the vivid talk beside her autumn fire. These and similar hospitalities gave us the pleasure of our last happy season by the North Shore— before the autumn of 1917 merged into the fateful winter of 1918.

CHAPTER NINETEEN

LIFE has its inevitable shadows, and into a period of unrelieved darkness our ship was now sailing. A long and dangerous illness confined my husband during the months of that winter, and just as the issue of the war was at its desperate moment of crisis my sister Rose died, after a week's illness, in California. *Dies Iræ* indeed were those days when my only child's life also hung in the balance, and that of my husband, as I was told by consulting physicians, was dangerously uncertain.

Reviewing my own life and the gifts of opportunity so lavishly bestowed, my greatest gratitude lies in the recognition of the characters of the remarkable personalities who were my parents, my sister, and my husband. Words of extraordinary imagination and instinct are even now repeated to me by friends who heard them from the lips of my mother, who, although a remarkable example of the persistence of Puritan traditions, was possessed of a delightful wit and as delightful a sympathy for many whose lives and characters were totally different from her own. "Southern women, my dear," she once said to me, "marry for money and never regret it." "Look at your room after your guests have left it," was another word of advice to a young housekeeper; a hint of arrangement of rooms which might well be re-

239

membered. And although not worldliness but other-worldliness was her constant aim and desire, the loyal wife of her politician husband spoke with a flash of her delicious humor when she said to my sister when she married a Democrat, "You may change your religion if you choose, but I would never forgive you if you changed your politics." Of my father I have so fully written that no further words are necessary to express my love and my gratitude.

My husband, who combined the excellent traditions of his parents with his great musical talent, inherited also the de Koven humor. His gifts as a potential comedian made him as perfect a *raconteur* of stories, in all accents and dialects, as his contemporaries ever heard, and to these gifts was added a heart devoid of *rancune* and a simplicity as wholly devoid of pose or pretension. Too few were the periods when his hero-ically followed career left him free to relax into moods of happy comradeship and the wit and gayety of which he was so delightfully a master. His long activity as a musical critic, for which he was unusually well equipped, gave him much satisfaction. He received unvarying appreciation for his just and sympathetic commentaries from all the singers and instrumentalists who passed before him. His literary style, developed by his Oxford studies, was clear and balanced and sometimes eloquent. According to Abbey and Grau, as well as Hammerstein and Campanini, his criticisms were considered authori-tative by all the singers.

Of the surviving members of my beloved family I may speak but briefly. My sister and I are blessed with children and grandchildren. My brother and his wife, who has inherited much of Dolly Madison's wit, much of her mother's beauty, with a courage and loyalty all her own, live near me in their beautiful Long Island house. In Lake Forest, nephews and nieces, with their little children, make for me a home atmosphere tender and consoling. A new house has arisen on the ashes of our beloved old home, which burned with all its contents on a winter night of 1920. But children still play by the little lake and Fairlawn is still lovely with flowers and the old trees of our youth. My daughter, who has inherited some of my father's traits, some of her own father's, with a great keenness of perception, has a justice and loyalty which make her the best friend of all. Sometimes she and her husband with their little boys consent to spend some months in my house, which is far too empty without them. Of my sister Rose I may speak and try to leave a faint picture of their mother for her children. She was the jewel in the matrix, the concentrated combination of the traits of our parents. She was typically Western in her freedom from self-consciousness, as fresh and invigorating in her indomitable joy of life as a sunlit prairie morning. That aristocracy of good instinct was exemplified in my parents, whose origin, from long-descended English stock, was clearly indicated in voice and manner and in invariable kindness and simplicity. My sister's kindness of heart, her large tolerance, never needed the usual development of experience. She may have listened to my father's instruction, "never to say anything about anyone if you have nothing pleasant to say," but I doubt if she did, for she followed this rule instinctively from childhood. A perfect listener, she was also, from earliest childhood, practicing that ultimate social accomplishment as if she had been an inheritor of centuries of French tradition. She carried her perfect little head high and nobly like my father. Like a tall flower I see her in all the numberless mind pictures of which she is the center. Hazel eyes, under the brows of my father, gazed with riveted attention upon each comrade, and, with a smile of such exquisite sweetness as we shall never again see, her face seemed to blossom into sheer loveliness and realize every dream. A radiance indescribable shone from that face of spring, and Flora incarnate seemed to walk before us. No hint of calculation was ever discoverable in any thought or act of her life, and the beauty which was the gift of nature was equaled by a joy-bringing disposition no less remarkable. Her mind was clear and vividly impressionable, her conclusions rapid and astonishingly correct, so that her advice, which was never tinged with sentimentality, was excellent. Her literary taste was discriminating and she was her husband's best critic. As a critic of humanity she was tolerant and yet expert, with the experience of the multitude of relationships which were offered to her triumphant beauty and were retained by the pure sunlight of the happiness which she radiated, the keen appreciation and loyal friendship which she bestowed. "I saw your sister pass in the street," one disappointed, lonely woman said to me, "and the world seemed right in a moment." Such was my sister, the desire of all our hearts, who left life before the waning of her beauty and of whom it was

MRS. REGINALD DE KOVEN

MR. REGINALD DE KOVEN

said that she was "more regretted than anyone of all her day and region."

After my sister's death we spent the quietest of summers in Nahant while I struggled to regain my composure, tried to find my way out of the darkness of my agonized bereavement. A temporary improvement in my husband's health permitted him to begin, during the quiet winter of 1919, his last opera, that "Rip Van Winkle" which was produced in Chicago. He continued and finished this work during another quiet summer at Nahant, which was, indeed, a period of almost complete retirement from our usual occupations. In November, 1919, my husband went to Chicago to oversee the production of his opera. Tragedy, curiously complete as in a Greek drama, was played in this last act of his career. The opera had been commissioned by Campanini, but he died three weeks before its production. My husband was unbearably overstrained by the disintegration of the company, which entailed his own supervision of chorus and principals, lighting and stage management. He was also faced with the business manager's ultimatum to produce the opera with only six rehearsals. Determined to avoid the responsibility of certain disaster, Hasselmans, the able French conductor, threw down his *bâton* after the rehearsal of only one act. Another, far less able, conductor was supplied, and by reason of the enthusiastic co-operation of the singers the opera miraculously achieved success. A second performance was far better. For the third representation which was thrown open to the general public the house was sold out. So did the American public show its interest in the opera, an interest never manifested for any similar American production in our country.

I had been present at the first performance and had returned to New York. A telegram from my husband announced, "House sold out for Friday night, box office *Vox Dei* Hurrah." It was his last word to me. That evening, January 16, 1920, as he was talking of his next work, he sank into unconsciousness. One performance of the work which had been approved of by the American public in Chicago was given in New York. But in the Lexington Opera House, whose echoes imperatively demand at least one orchestral rehearsal, none was accorded. No rehearsal for chorus or principals and no opportunity given for the critics to hear the complete opera. But in spite of the fact that the orchestration was inevitably and seriously harmed by the interfering echoes in the opera house, the public was pleased and the critics only displeased, and naturally, with the orchestral misrepresentation.

When Mr. Kahn could, lately and publicly, declare in my hearing that "Our American opera house should no longer be used as a stalking place for any American opera," no comment is necessary. The records of financial and critical approbation which accompanied the production of Reginald de Koven's two operas in New York and Chicago exist and can be examined by any who wish to be acquainted with the facts. The American public will not see another American opera at the Metropolitan during Mr. Gatti's management, according to his own pronouncement. His intention to produce American works, carried out with several operas, met, according to his observation to my husband, its greatest obstacle in the hostility of the American critics. This hostility was not shown in their treatment of "The Canterbury Pilgrims." The persistent adherence of Mr. Gatti in his determination not to revive this opera has been continued in spite of the protests of many of the personnel of the Metropolitan Company and of some of the conductors. The Italians in Italy declare that they control our opera houses. It is no vain boast.

Five years have gone by since the curtain fell on my life with my husband. In a country where there is no leisure from business and its absorbing and existing occupations, the men die too soon. I have thus been companioned in my widowhood by almost all of my friends and contemporaries. I have had to face the same problem of readjustment to a new life of solitude, had to find, like my friends, my own way out of the shadows. The presence in my house of Sir Oliver Lodge and his wife, for a few weeks in the winter of my husband's death, was of deep interest and consolation. I investigated the published records of that new scientific inquiry regarding the survival of personality and, like many who have made that investigation without prejudice, have been convinced that this is reasonably established.

A journey to England in 1920 gave me the opportunity to ask Professor McDougall, then Professor of Psychology at Oxford and president of the English Society for Psychical Research, to accept the same position in the American society. This privilege was in-

trusted to me by the trustees of the latter society. So
on a journey to Oxford, where I visited my husband's
college, I had an interview with Professor McDougall,
whose interest in the movement, although later separated from the American society, is still active and at
the point of initiating a new society in Boston. The
horizon of one who believes he has seen authentic
glimpses of a continuing life is wider, is happier, than
that of the skeptic. The ethical content implicit in the
messages which reach us is logical in its agreement with
instinct and practice. All earthly griefs and disappointments are reduced to a relative significance and all fear
of death is removed. The value of such conclusions, the
help in such perceptions, need no argument. Thus
fortified, I have borne that *juste et profonde douleur
de l'apparente separation* of which Maeterlinck wrote
in his profoundly beautiful letter of consolation after
my husband's death. At a luncheon in my house, in
company with Lady Glenconner, only two days before,
he had spoken of death and its mystery, and with a wide
knowledge of the related subjects had discussed with my
other friends the phenomena called psychic. "To you,"
he wrote also, "who know that Death's Empire is not
great, I will write none of the usual words of consolation." Consolation I needed, none the less, and found
it after long months, even years, in the impersonal
rapture of the contemplation of nature and of its reflection in art. In Egypt, I found the meaning of the
poet's word "timeless," breathing the calm which floats
in every desert breeze, heeding the significance of the

246

immemorial temples, with their shrines for the oft returning soul, the Ka of the Egyptians.

"The light which never was on sea or land" illumines
those Egyptian skies whose dawning and dying glories
I watched, I listened to, as to symphonies of recurring
music. I seemed to live on a super-terrestrial plane in
Egypt, entered into what might almost be called the
fourth dimension, where perceptions are immeasurably
extended. There also I seemed to explore the un-
plumbed depths of time, in the monuments to the ancient
Gods, and in that strange survival and mixture of
humanity which exists in Cairo. On the day I visited
the City of Tombs I passed a blazing merry-go-round
of Arab children whose azure and scarlet rags whirled
pennants of recurring gayety, of eternally renewed life,
against mountainous débris of fallen palaces. It was
a Friday, the Moslem's Sabbath, and the sand-brown
streets, between the closed doors of the mute houses, was
a thoroughfare for the pilgrims to this mortuary citadel.
Here alone, in all the realm of Islam, lingers from the
Egyptians a faith in the return of the spirit, and here
families come to commune, on stated days, in the houses
prepared for them, with the dead. On one roadside
corner I passed a fanatic intoning the Koran, and a
prostrate woman, with a black veil over her head, singing
a dirge; a blind man cried out his evening prayer to a
muezzin tower; a beggar shrieked imprecations at my
passing; and crossing before me was a girl whose oblique
glance from brown eyes of romance hinted of Arabian
nights of love and moonlight. Against the Moorish
arches figures of manly youth, clad in white and tur-

baned, stood out in remembered poses of unconsciously perfect pictorial composition, and always there were children laughing merrily and calling out from the brown doorways to the strangers. The depths of humanity here threw up their age-old types, recurring, unchangeable past the centuries.

In the streets and bazaars of the town I mingled in the torrent of Arabians, of Sudanese, of all the strange visitors from the desert, of veiled women, water-carriers, and pigeon-venders, which pours in a never-tiring movement, a sort of mob excitement, gregarious and instinctive as that of a herd of animals or a swarm of bees. I found the response in these Oriental members of the human family strangely courteous, instantaneously comprehending of my unspoken observation. One exquisite young lad, with the curled auburn head seen sometimes among the Arabs, smiled brilliantly, even lovingly, in response to an admiring glance. "Sayeda" (a lady), a ragged woman exclaimed as I stepped from my carriage. And as for seductive grace and manner I never met the equal of "the cousin" of the proprietor of a little shop of antiquities who strolled in from the street to help me in my purchases. With a face like the moon at its full, under locks curled and perfumed like a courtier from the vanished palaces of Al Raschid, he spoke his fluent French with a grace of gesture as rhythmical as that of any *jeune premier* of a Parisian stage or *salon*. And this courtesy of an old race was most perfectly exemplified in Abdul, my dragoman, who, with the same rhythmic grace of bearing, a wit and

MY HOUSE IN ITALY

gayety and a real "intelligence of heart," was as great a gentleman as I have ever seen in any drawing-room.

Shall I speak of the yellow sea of the Sakkara Desert with its tombs and its pyramid profiles against the mauve skies? Shall I recall the moon disk of silver over the golden hills which rise beyond the city—purer silver, purer gold than seen elsewhere? Shall I speak of the wonders of Cairo's four hundred mosques, far more varied and infinitely more beautiful in pierced stone windows, in carved lattices, in inlaid walls of turquoise and lapis lazuli than those of Constantinople? Not half has been written of these Oriental monuments by Egyptian travelers; not a hint except in two little monographs by a French lady, who was my guide, has been given to the Western world of the unmined treasure of history which these mosques suggest and preserve. The stories of the Princesses of these Moslem harems and palaces are full of tragic drama. The "Pearl" princess, Shaggaret et Dur, is buried in a little mosque tomb as white and delicately carved as the stone lace of Spain, and her story is as red as the heart of a pomegranate. How she came to rule over the palace of the Caliph, her husband; how she killed him and then murdered the lover whom she had raised to her side; how she was herself done to death under the painted slippers of her handmaidens— is material poignant enough to tempt the moderns who, like Bourget, seek for new subjects in a new world. The old world, whose broken fragments gleam like spilled jewels in the brown deserts of Cairo's streets of the dead, are there to be gathered up into crowns for any writer.

Denderah was the first visited Egyptian temple. Here, as in a symphony, the themes of love and immortality are wrought out in its goddess pillars, in the mounting stair processionals, in the pizzicatos of delicate decorations, in flower friezes, reed dados, bird haunted, hymning the beauty of earth and of heaven. And was I not carried to the shrine by four bearers, singing the same chant of triumph which accompanied the ancient kings on their pilgrimages?

Karnak, seen first by the stars whose necklaces glittered around the tops of the pillars, I remember with thoughts touched to the deepest emotion, and I remember also the wings of the little birds flying over the sacred lake of the Moon Goddess. A still deeper memory is the silence of the royal gods at Luxor, under the moonlight, their hands on their knees, their eyes set in a clairvoyant dream of Eternity, initiates in its mystery. The violet light on the river and on the treasure mountains of the Valley of the Kings I can still see, can hear the songs of the boatmen as I walked by the riverside in those days of forgetfulness of human grief, of any self-pity, lost as I was in the spectacle of beauty eternal, of life recurring. And so in Egypt I was reborn and am living a sort of postscript to my normal life of activity, of association with my husband and with his never abandoned hopes and plans. Sicily, Greece, Constantinople, and Spain I have also visited, and the beautiful Loire with its châteaux.

I have also had the courage to return to my own country, and in my New York house, without my musician, have attempted to conform to the traditions of the musical center he established when we were young and together. I delight, as always, in the thrill of our great brilliant city with its vitalizing sea air and its rush of triumphant prosperity. I visit the public schools, carrying, like a book agent, my little work on Citizenship, born of a talk with Mr. Arnold Foster (nephew of the poet Arnold) at Nauheim; an attempt to provide an American primer like the book on the same subject he had written. The Arnold heart was nearly at its last beat; my own in the summer of 1908 was so weak that I was warned that it would not last out the year, yet in the spring of 1925 it still marks the passing of time, still holds its long recollections, still rejoices in friends loving and loyal with life-long comradeship and with that deepening appreciation, that consoling intimacy of good opinion, we may hope to merit.

Each spring I return to my house in Italy. Among all the generations of the lovers of Florence I feel that I am also an inheritor of its gifts to humanity, have my own debt of gratitude for those brief weeks of my early happiness, my own share in its beauty. Another villa is mine where, from a flower-grown terrace, I watch the sun as it sets behind the same purple mountains, where nightingales sing in another garden, and a chime of bells at evening rings its immortal message. An evening mood, a piece, full of promise I find in the long twilights, and something of that continuing rapture in beauty of which the New England sage spoke, in his eightieth year, to the friend of my youth. And in this evening mood the shadows grow clearer and like distant music fade in harmony. A longer, clearer perspective than in passionate youth is defined in these lingering lines, and the streets of an aërial city lead beyond the pointing cypresses into the sunset. The heart grown responsive to all human contacts holds its deep consolations, values grow clearer, vision grows wider and "the way winds upward, yes, to the very end."

INDEX

Abbey & Grau, 170, 240
Abbott, Margaret, 138
Abbott, Mrs. Mary, 137–138
Acres, Bob, 100
Adamowski, 170
Adams, Charles Francis, 201
Adams, Henry, 200–201
Aix-les-Bains, 223
Albemarle, Duke of, 1
Aldrich, Senator Nelson, 74–76, 188
Allison, Senator, 188
"Amazons, The," 93
Ames, Oakes, 35–36
Ancona, 215
Anethan, Baron d', 129
Angell, Phoebe, 17
Arles, 224
Arlington Hotel, 50, 66–67, 74–75
Armorer's Song, 135
Armour, Ogden, 184
Arnold, Matthew, 84
Arthur, President, 53, 65, 68, 73
Astor, Helen, 128
Astor, Mrs. John Jacob, 90, 182
Astor, Waldorf, 145
"As You Like It," 134
Austria, 48
Avignon, 224

Barbizon School, 42
Barnaby, 133, 135, 145
Bar Harbor, 83
Barrett, Wilson, 132, 210
Bates, Linden, 38
Bayard, Miss, 68
Baylies, Mrs., 182
Beale, General, 54
Beale, Miss Emily, 67, 68
Beale, Mrs., 53
Beatty, Admiral, 14
Beerbohm, Max, 180
"Begum, The," 123–126, 127
Belasco, David, 149
Bell, Digby, 124

Bellevue Place, 132
Belmont, Mrs. August, 82, 90, 166
Benton, Mrs., 58
Benton, Thomas H., 59
Berry, Judge, 191
Beveridge, Senator Albert, 188, 198
Biglow Papers, 96
Biography of Paul Jones, 201, 207–213, 214
Blaine, James G., 34, 41
Blaine, Mrs. James G., 53, 64
Blarney Castle, 48
Boccaccio, 44
Bodansky, Arturo, 231
"Bohemian Girl, The," 133
Boston Ideals, The, 132
Bostonians, The, 132
Botta, Mrs., 43, 46
Bourget, Paul, 186
Boutwell, Mr., 33
Bowen, Mrs. *See* de Koven, Louise
Brady, Rev. Cyrus Townsend, 211
Braze, Mrs., 182
Breese, Mr., 177
Brema, Marie, 173
Brewster, General, 65, 66
Brooke, Lady. *See* Warwick, Lady
Brooks, James, 35, 36
Browning, 100, 181
Browning Class, 99, 100
Brunswick Hotel, 142
Bryan, W. J., 139–141
Bryce, Lord, 110
Bryn Mawr, 215
Buchanan, President, 72, 73
Buckingham Palace, 152
Buell, A. C., 207–209, 211, 213
Burgoyne, 108
By the Waters of Babylon, 195

Calvé, Madame Emma, 171, 172
Cambon, Jules, 128, 187, 189, 191
Cameron, Mrs., 54, 64
"Camille," 177

253

INDEX

INDEX

INDEX

256

INDEX

INDEX

INDEX

Shubert brothers, 217
Siddall, Elizabeth, 179
"Siegfried," 54, 180
Sloane, Mrs. Henry, 182
Smalley, 147
Smith, Mr. Ballard, 156
Smith, George, 8
Smith, Harry, 98, 124, 130, 133–135,
   145, 193, 217
Smith, Mary Eveline, 18
Somersetshire, 1
South Williamstown, 15–17
Spofford, Mr., 44
Stafford House, 1
St. Andrews Club, 183
Starrett, Mrs., 136
Sterner, Albert, 98

Stone, Herbert, 138
Stone, Melville, 138
Strauss, 127
Studdford, Grace, 194
Stuttgart, 92, 127
Swinburne, 181
Switzerland, 48
Sykes, Jerome, 193–194

Talleyrand, 91
Talleyrand, Comtesse de, 92
Tamames, Duca di, 185
Taylor, Mr. Chatfield, 99
Taylor, Mrs. Chatfield, 153, 174, 183,
   221
Tempest, Marie, 161, 173–175
Terry, Ellen, 178, 180
Tetrazzini, 215
Thibault, M., 187
Thursfield, Mr., 211
Tildsley, Dr., 122
Times, London, 129, 211
Toscanini, 228
Toulouse, 224
Townsend, Mrs., 187
Tree, Sir Herbert, 174
Tree, Lady, 174
Tremont Theater, 154
"Tristan and Isolde," 172
Tun Moat, 2

Vanderbilt, Mrs. W. K., Jr., 68
Van Alen, Mr., 155
Vetsera, Baroness, 131

Vevey, 81, 216, 221–222
Victoria, Queen, 150
Vienna, 127–131
Villa Camerata, 92–94
Villa Hermosa, Marchesa de, 185
Villard, Mr., 143
Virgil, 16
Von Koven. *See* de Koven, name
Von Suppé, 127

Waddington, Mr. and Mrs., 152
Wadsworth, Mrs., 89
Wagner, 125, 130, 180
Wagner, Lizzie, 25
Wallace, Mr. and Mrs., 226
Ward, Charles, 37
Ward, Mrs. Humphry, 104
Warner, Charles Dudley, 104
Warwick, Lady, 151
Washington (city), 7–8, 33–36, 50–70,
   186–206
Washington's bodyguard, 3
Western Magazine, 136
Westminster, 3–4
Wetmore, Senator, 188
Wetmore, Mrs., 187
Wheeler, Mr., 33–34
White, Josephine, 38
White, Stanford, 176, 185
White, Mrs. Stanford, 177
Whitney, Mrs., 158
Wilde, Oscar, 145–148, 179
Williams, Robert, 72
Wilson, Francis, 132
Wilson, Miss, 57
Wilson, Secretary, 226
Wilson, Woodrow, 197–198
Winthrop, John Still, 87
Winthrop, Margaret, 91
Wolcott, Senator, 188
Woolf, 168–169
World, New York, 156, 176
World's Fair, 185
Wrenn, Bob, 184
Wrenn, Everts, 184
Wu, Mrs., 57
Wyndham, 146

Yans, Anneke, 216
Ysaye, 173, 192
Yznaga, Consuelo, 43
Yznaga, Mrs., 177